# International Lighting Design

by V. Lorenzo Porcelli,

Donna Green and the editors of

First published in the United States of
America by:
Rockport Publishers, Inc.
P.O. Box 396 · Five Smith Street
Rockport, Massachusetts 01966
Telephone: (508) 546-9590
Telex: 5106019284
Fax: (508) 546-7141

Distributed to the book trade and art trade
in the U.S. and Canada by:
North Light, an imprint of
Writer's Digest Books
1507 Dana Avenue
Cincinnati, Ohio 45207
Telephone: (513) 531-2222

Distributed to the book trade and art trade
throughout the rest of the world by:
Hearst Books International
105 Madison Avenue (20th floor)
New York, New York 10016
Telephone: (212) 481-0355

Other Distribution by:
Rockport Publishers, Inc.
Rockport, Massachusetts 01966

Printed in Singapore

# Contents

# Selected Works

A26 by Miles Keller
Acheo by Gianfranco Frattini
Aerial by Ron Arad
Aero by James Evanson
AeTo by Fabio Lombardo
Altair by Garcia Garay
Altalena by Sant and Bigas
Andrea by Andrzej Duijas
Antinous by Studio Naço
Ara by Philippe Starck
Arcade by Roberto Marcatti
Ares by Roberto Marcatti
Argo by Richard Sapper
BaKa-Rú by Ingo Maurer
  and team
Bali by Luciano Pagani
Balisk by Morphosis
Barking Dog By Morphosis
Burlington Desk Light by
  David Morgan
Café Olé by Roberto Marcatti
Chicago Tribune by Matteo
  Thun
China by Stephan Copeland
Chip Wall Sconce by Piotr
  Sierakowski
Ciclos by Michele de Lucchi
Circus by Roberto Marcatti
City View Lighthouses by
  James Evanson
Comoda by Eros Bollani
Crystal Needle by Terence Main
Dancing Angel by Morphosis
Dea by Tiziano Cuberli
Dede by Enzo Berti
DeLight by Stiletto Studios
Dinosaur II by Pascal Luthi
Dove by Barbaglia and Colom
Dynamite by Jan van
  Opzeeland
Eclipse by Mario Bellini
Eco by Barbaglia and Colombo
El Globo by Studio Naço
Elroy by Liz Galbraith
Erco Oseris by Ambasz and
  Piretti
Ettore by Ernesto Gismondi
Expanded Line by King and
  Miranda
Feather by Robert Sonneman
Fenix by Garcia Garay
Floor Lamp by Whitney Boin
Floor Lamp by Lee Weitzman
Floor Lamp No. 1 and 2 by
  Robert Silance
Flut by Erio Bosi
Focus by Bruno Gecchelin
Formosa by Marcatti & Crotti
Four Button by Mark Parrish
Frankfurt by Pep Sant and
  Ramón Bigas
Galileo by Gavin Steer
Gavina by Josep Llusca
Grall System by Ferrari, Pagani
  and Perversi Assoc.
Grip 36 by Gary Payne
Guardian by Robly A. Glover Jr.
Halo-Click by Sottsass Associati
Halogen Floor Lamp by Mike
  Nuttall
Halogen Lamp by Eric Margry
  Design
Hanger by Michael Pinkus
Henri by Jerry Ketel
Heron by Samual Ribet
Homage To Moholy Nagy by
  Studio Naço
Hopper by Peter Krouwel
Iló-Ilú by Ingo Maurer and
  team
Joia by Josep Llusca
Karl and Freddy by Red Square

La Lune Sans Le Chapeau by
  Phillipe Starck
Lamp #1 by Lawrence Laske
Lashtal Sconce by Beckmann
  and Esrafily
Lazylight by Paolo Francesco
Lester 220 by Vico Magistretti
Light Tapestry by Jerome H.
  Simon
Lighted By The Blinds by
  Terence Leong
Lighten Up by Mark Parrish
Lighthouse by Frederic
  Schwartz
Lippa by Maurizio Bertoni
Logo by Barbaglia and
  Columbo
Lucy and Tania by Harvey
  Mackie
Luminous Chair by Kyrre
  Andersen
Luna by Josep Llusca
Luna Pendant by Kevin von
  Kluck
Lunatica by Donatella Costa
Lyra by Giuseppe Raimondi
M6 by Jan Van Lierde
Mackinaw 900 by Larry Lazin
Manhattan Series by Blaich
  and Van Elk
Mask by David Potter
Maya by Daniel T. Ebihara
Mercur by Vladimir Pezdirc
Mikado by Ferdinand A
  Porsche
Modi: Terra by Toshiyuki Kita
Moontower by Paul Ruine
Motorized Robotic by
  Shiu-Kay Kan
Motto Yubi by Robert
  Sonneman
Ms. Dee Dee Deluxe by
  David Gale
Nessie by De Pas, D'Urbino
  and Lomazzi
Nest by Kyrre Andersen
Night Shades by Ulrich Hoereth
On Taro Giro by Toshiyuki Kita
On-Off by Meda, Raggi
  and Santachiara
Orbit by Peter Krouwel
Palio by King and Miranda
Pantograph by Michel Dallaire
Papiro by Sergio Calatroni
Pendant by Frederick Ramond
Pi by Jan Van Lierde
Picchio by Isao Hosoe
Piramide by Marco Pasanella
Plana by Carlo Urbinati Ricci
Pocket Lamp by Judith van
  Brunschot
Poe by Giugiaro Design
Polyphemus Flashlight by
  Emilio Ambasz
Quahog by Leo Blackman
Ready Made by David Palterer
Regina by Jorge Pensi
Rinascimento by Matteo Thun
Rock-it by Alex Mayer

Saeta by Josep Llusca
Sail by Kyrre Andersen
Sail by Miles Keller
Sapiens by Sacha Ketoff
Sardine by Viemeister and
  Krohn
Satelight by Stiletto Studios
SB-16 Spacebird by Kenneth
  Kane
Scaragoo by Stefan Lindfors
Sciopticon by Hans Ansems
Serena by Robert Wendrich
Serpentina by Johannes
  Peter Klien
Sette Magie by Lella and
  Massimo Vignelli
Shaman by Alex Locadia
Sigla 1 by René Kemna
Sini 1 by René Kemna
SL48 Solar Lantern by
  Moggridge Associates
Soffio by Emilio Ambasz
Squale by Studio Naço
Squish by Fabio Di Bartolomei
Star by Roberto Pamio
Starry Skies by Frederic
  Schwartz
Stasis by Ralph Osterhout
Strala by Laughton and Deacon
Swag by Sinya Okayama
Table Lamp by Trivedi
  and Munshi
Taraxacum by Achille
  Castiglione
Tata by Eros Bollani
Tender by Michele De Lucchi
3i by Thomas Eisl
Tikal by P.G. Ramella
Tilt 36 by Doyle Crosby
Tiramisú by Roberto Marcatti
Titania By Meda and Rizzatto
Tolomeo by De Lucchi
  and Fassina
Tom by Ezio Bellini
Tower 001 by Maurizio Favetta
Transform Lamps by Red
  Square
Trio by Vladimir Pezdirc
Tris Tras by King and Miranda
Tulip by Ronald Reyburn
U19 Floor Lamp by
  RandallToltzman
Uchida Lamp by Shigeru
  Uchida
Urania by Garcia Garay
Upside Down by Jan Van
  Lierde
Urushi by Toshiyuki Kita
Ventosa by Roberto Marcatti
Verte A and Verte P by
  Sergi Devesa
Via by Bruck of West Germany
Victory by De Pas, D'Urbino
  and Lomazzi
Vienna 1900 by Robert
  Sonneman
Voyagers by Alex Locadia
Wall Sconce by Kevin Farrell
Wall Sconces by Margry
  and Anderson
Winged Victory by David Baird
Yanagi by Masciocchi Merich
YaYaHo by Ingo Maurer and
  team
Zag by Paul Ruine
Zefiro by P.G. Ramella

*International Lighting Design* is a book that visually celebrates the best and brightest in lighting from around the world. From the boldly futuristic Space II to the ergonomically sound Illuminated Magnifier, from the grandly innovative ArenaVision to the sculpturally poised Fantomas, the lighting presented here conveys the eclectic design spirit of the eighties.

Selected from over 400 examples of lighting submitted to Design Publications in New York over the course of 1989, this book offers a comprehensive overview of contemporary luminaires. Its pages are filled with images of more than 180 outstanding lighting projects designed over the past five years, each one chosen because of its unique contribution to the state of the art. In addition, *International Lighting Design* features eleven behind-the-scene case studies that focus on special lighting projects from the United States, Japan, the

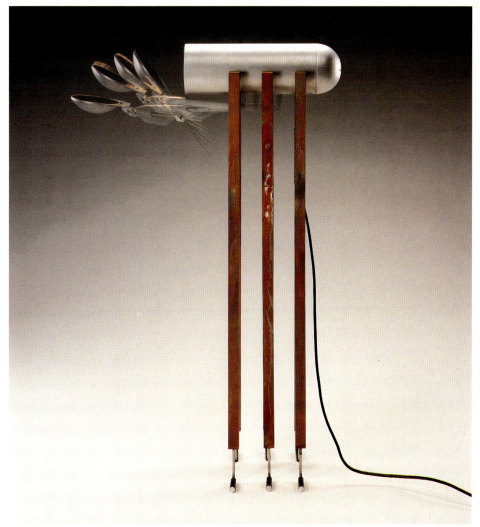

*Barking Dog by Morphosis interacts to programmed signals by barking and then opening a flap to expose its light source.*

Netherlands, Belgium, Italy and Switzerland. Interviews with the design teams and studies of their sketches and engineering drawings offer unique insights into the creative process.

It is barely one hundred years since Thomas Edison's 1879 discovery of electricity. Since then the light bulb has played a revolutionary role in our everyday lives, illuminating our homes and workplaces, controlling our moods and perceptions. Yet lighting now has novel connotations and this, in part, can be attributed to significant changes in technology.

Sophisticated remote control systems and sensory electronics, for example, allow designers today to create lights that automatically move, activate, dim and even "talk." Another important new influence is the small but powerful halogen bulb which enables designers to create lamps that burn brightly without necessarily being big, suggesting in some cases that lighting and its electrical components can be touched and manipulated safely. Solid-state electroluminescent panels offer unprecedented dimensions to night lighting and signage; many of today's designers are inventively incorporating this technology in their work. Lasers, fiber optics and holography also offer enormous potential in their ability to

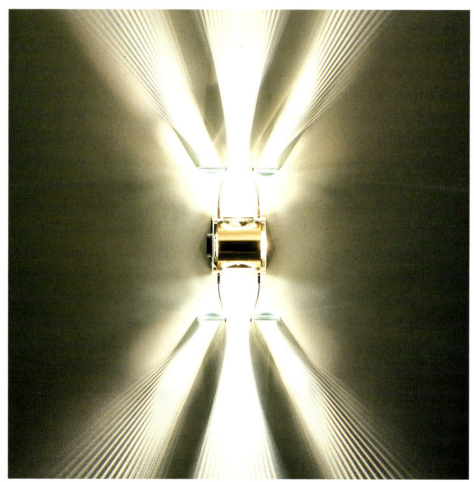

*Light Tapestry by Jerome Simon houses a halogen bulb in a tiny metal enclosure.*

project and manipulate light, although these possibilities have yet to be incorporated commercially in mainstream lighting design.

But not all the lighting to be seen in *International Lighting Design* is a direct result of fast-paced changes in technology. Contemporary lighting designers are busy experimenting with a variety of unconventional materials to diffuse and reflect light, creating unique environments in the process. Glass, however, remains the material synonymous with lighting and

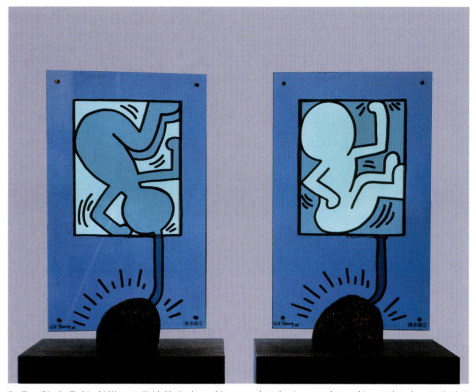

*On Taro Giro by Toshiyuki Kita sets Keith Haring's graphics on an electroluminescent plate, making art that glows in the dark.*

numerous designs in this book brilliantly explore its transparency and opacity. Many designers are also producing lamps that follow strict ergonomic criteria derived from extensive research into user requirements, while other designers are creating a wide range of lamps that offer multiple functions. And in the fashionable spirit of historicism, some designs pay homage to past styles, while others take their cue from traditional crafts.

Embracing all these different trends, *International Lighting Design* presents the variegated visions of designers, artists, architects and engineers working around the world. Track systems and spotlights, desk lamps and floor lamps, task lights and sconces: the designs here range from the functional to the avant-garde. Indeed, *International Lighting Design* gives us a glimpse not only of contemporary lighting but also of the work of designers who will be responsible for the way our environments are lit in the twenty-first century.

—*Donna Green*

---

*Special acknowledgement and thanks go to a number of people who were involved in putting this book together: to Amy Ancona for her tireless research and caption writing; to the editors of* International Design Magazine, *Annetta Hanna, Chee Pearlman and Nick Backlund; to Jennifer Domer for her innovative art direction; to designer Robert Rainey and art assistant Jacqueline Thaw; and, finally, to Steven Frank for creating the index.*

No one I know seriously uses the term "good design" anymore; how quaint that expression now seems with all its precious connotations. Instead, design is perhaps best seen as something substantive, something that belongs to the real nature of a thing. It was with this in mind that we set about compiling *International Lighting Design*, a book about lighting of the mid- to late eighties—so don't look for any "good design" endorsements in this book. Rather, view *International Lighting Design* as a unique release of design energy that explores divergent directions, contradicting philosophies, sometimes irreverent analogies and metaphors, and makes asymmetrical the boundaries of art, craft and design.

Similarly, *International Lighting Design* is not a critique of lighting nor does it herald any particular movement. It is a book that presents lighting as a collection of ideas, images and philosophies from the present, past and future. On these pages are elements of Cubism, the machine shop ethic, NASA, Shaker design, jazz, Las Vegas, Calder, post-modernism, the Swiss grid, assemblage, Noguchi, performance art and Memphis. Indeed, a review of these pages reveals the multifarious dialects of design flourishing as never before.

Richard Sapper's 1972 Tizio lamp stands, to some degree, as the genesis of *International Lighting Design*. (Was the genesis of the Tizio the Luxo lamp of thirty-three years earlier?) Spindly, wispy, crisp, black and wonderfully animated, Tizio is an articulated task light with a halogen lamp. The splendid Tizio spawned an entire industry intent on being ingenious, inventive and witty, where the emphasis was more on how you did it (configu-

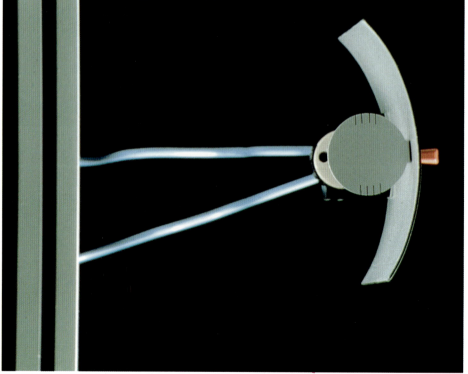

*Monolith Light by Brian Stewart*

ration) rather than what you did (illumination). The Tizio ushered in an endless array of

intriguing mechanisms and devices for articulating light that could support, move, position,

diffuse and radiate light in a myriad of gestures. The exuberance of its design spirit comman-

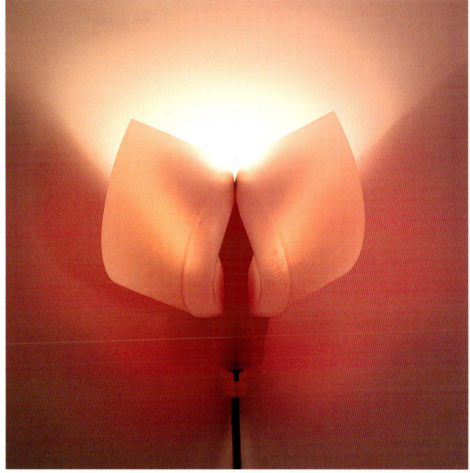

*by V. Lorenzo Porcelli*

*Ruby Begonia by Alec Drummond*

deered the minds of designers and encouraged them to explore, stretch and challenge their

perceptions of what lighting design can be.

*International Lighting Design* recognizes the advent of one-off lighting, or art light-

ing that is constructed not for commercial production but to create visual statements. There

was a time, not long ago, when industrial designers were reluctant to accept designs that

were not in full production — somehow these were seen as "ringers," off on the sidelines

somewhere, not following the same rules, not accredited players. It is precisely this group

that has given lighting design, particularly in America, a jolt of new energy. The question

"Is it art, is it craft or is it design?" now elicits the response "Who cares?" as long as the work

is substantive. What we call art lighting reflects not so much the entry of art or artists into

the lighting design world as it does the inclusion of the rest of the world into what is con-

sidered art. Perhaps the only thing that happens in art lighting that isn't apparent in produc-

tion lighting is the aesthetics of the actual design process: the very act of creation is essential.

*Eco by Mario Barbaglia and Marco Columbo*

There are many works in this book worthy of detailed discussion but I will comment on only a few of them; readers will carry on their own dialogues with those designs that correspond to their personal visions as they emerge.

The Cascading Sconce by Thomas Hucker reveals a pure lyricism. Is the form the narrative, or is the light the narrative? Is the light cutting metaphorically through the panels or are the panels shaping the light? The eye is driven relentlessly upwards and downwards in rhythmic succession, trying to determine what the designer's *process of design* was.

Ad hoc design is not a new idea, but when Alec Drummond uses a common and disposable material in his wall lamp Ruby Begonia, he creates a surprisingly voluptuous and organic form. Like a movie with a surprise ending you are captivated initially by the lamp's form and then are astonished to discover what its original life was. (I won't tell you here...)

The passion for design in the Italian national temperament is evidenced in the line of designs by PAF. Most of these designs are by the formidable team of Mario Barbaglia and Marco Columbo. The Dove lamp (probably second only to the Tizio in popularity), the Logo, the Edipo and the Eco testify not only to a love of design but also to the enlightened support given by Italian industrialists, a support that is not matched elsewhere.

The Monolith Light by Brian Stewart is made up of crisp, machined elements, one dominant, one subordinate. The lamp's low voltage wires are set in a random wavy pattern that suggests the flow of electric current. This design expresses a mastery of minimalist geometry, yet it isn't rigid or beyond metaphor.

Decorative thrown light is not a new concept in lighting design. This effect is often used by stage designers, for example, but nowhere does it take on the sense of orchestrated visual music more clearly than in Shigeru Uchida's lamp Dear Fausto. Even its tripoidal form suggests a music stand.

While there are many remarkable luminaires that are delicate in appearance, it is a pleasure to see something as sleek and muscular as the ArenaVision floodlight by Philips. This design is like a great sports car — powerful, well-built and absolutely wonderful to look at. ArenaVision is a professional luminaire on a grand scale.

Analogy and metaphor still contribute the most voltage to creativity. The principal for balancing cantilevered weights used in Richard Sapper's Tizio lamp, for example, can

*ArenaVision by Gerrit Arts*

also be seen in drawbridge design, border guard barriers and construction cranes. The mind works by association. And so, to apply a Japanese adage to the Tizio: "To surpass the master pays the debt of what he gave you." I hope you find many lively examples of this process in *International Lighting Design*.

# Dear Fausto

by Shegiru Uchida

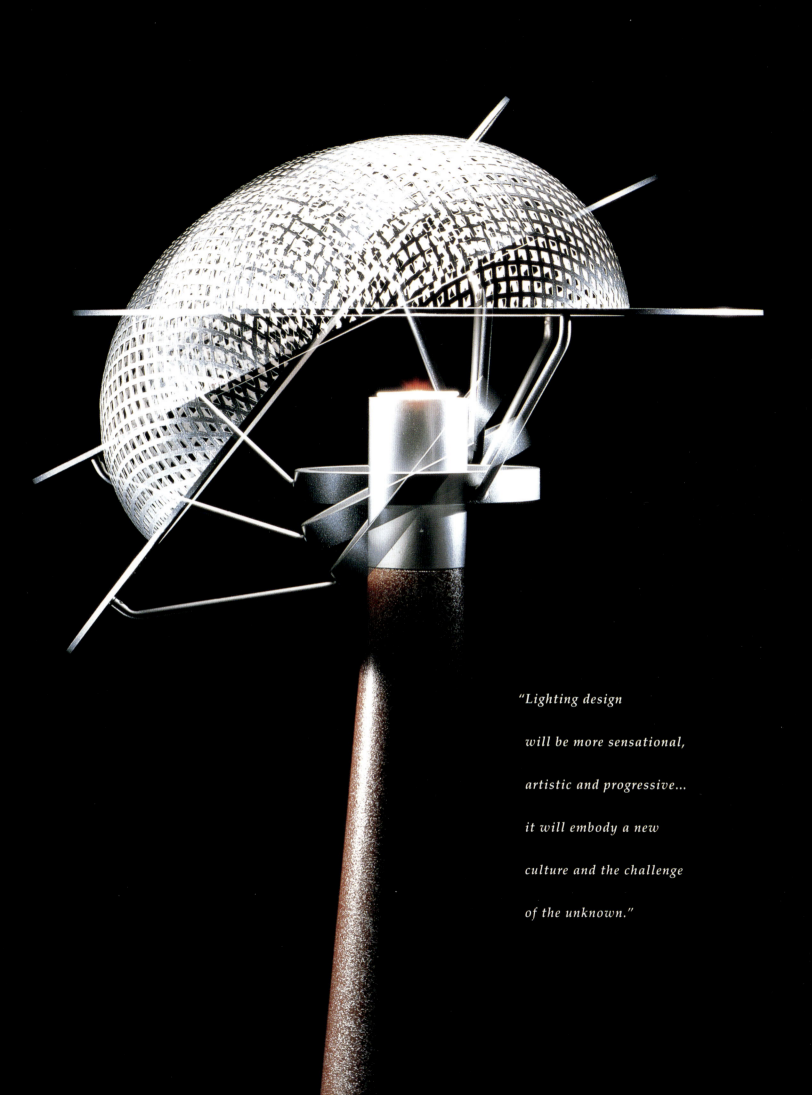

*"Lighting design*

*will be more sensational,*

*artistic and progressive...*

*it will embody a new*

*culture and the challenge*

*of the unknown."*

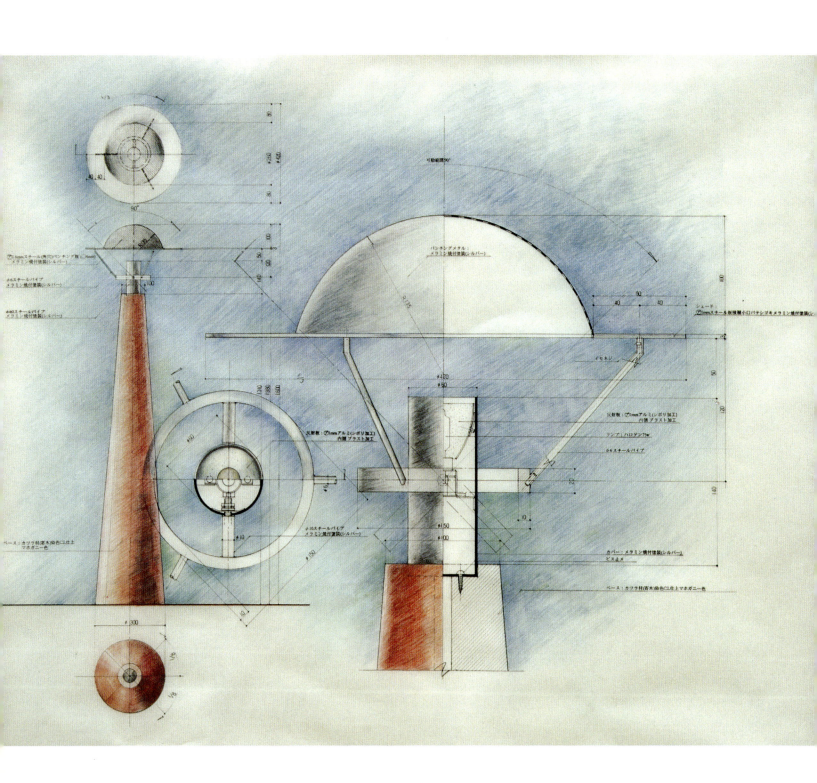

## Dear Fausto

**1988**
**Height 1600 mm x Diameter 300mm; Shade Diameter 420mm**

Casting splendid grids of light on the ceiling and walls, Dear Fausto is a halogen floor lamp designed by Shigeru Uchida of Studio 80, Tokyo, and named after Fausto, the son of Italian architect Aldo Rossi. The lamp stands tall and dignified; its impressive conical shaped support is fabricated from Katsura wood, its hooded reflector of square perforated steel with a baked melamine finish. The reflector, inspired by the brimmed hats Japanese school girls wear, tilts playfully from side to side, spreading light in all directions. The lamp was manufactured by the Yamagiwa Corporation, Tokyo, Japan.

# Interview

*Born in Yokohama, Japan in 1943, Shigeru Uchida graduated from Kuwasawa Design School in 1966. Along with his wife, Ikuyo Mitsuhashi and Toru Nishioka, two of Tokyo's outstanding designers, Uchida established Studio 80 in Tokyo in 1981. Uchida has designed a number of Issey Miyake and Yohji Yamamoto clothing stores in Japan as well as Charivari in New York and Maxfield in Los Angeles. In 1988 his "September" armchair became part of the permanent design collection at the Metropolitan Museum of Art in New York.*

**How was the project initiated?** The project was initiated by Yamagiwa Corporation, which asked me to design some lamps for their new collection. **How were you influenced or inspired?** At the time I was working on a hotel called Il Palazzo in Fukuoka, Japan. The hotel was designed by Aldo Rossi and my role was as an interior designer and an executive art director. Il Palazzo is like a medieval mansion and I wanted to create a lamp that would fit into this historical setting. At the same time I was inspired by the image of a girl wearing a hat. **Did you use any special materials or technology?** The halogen lamp cover needed to be small in diameter to fit the aesthetic configuration of the lamp, yet we also had to maintain low heat conductivity. Finally, after many experiments, we chose a 60mm diameter lamp cover made of steel pipe with a baked melamine finish, and a 75-wwatt halogen bulb. An aluminum reflective plate inside the post helps scatter the light. **What was the biggest obstacle?** Maintaining low heat conductivity. **What alternatives were explored?** We explored fabricating the lamp out of iron or marble. We now seek ways of producing the lamp more efficiently and less expensively. **What would you like to design next?** I would like to design many new products, not only from the point of view of an interior designer but also from the point of view of an industrial designer. **What is the future in lighting design?** Design, in general, will travel down two contrasting streams. One stream will carry a standardized design that is practical, simple, clean and flexible. The other stream will be more sensational, artistic and progressive. I prefer the latter because for me it embodies a new culture and the challenge of the unknown—there will be a lot to explore down this exciting stream.

*Ready Made*

**1985**
400mm x 200mm x 200mm

This composition of metal industrial components incorporating an exposed incandescent bulb was designed by David Palterer, Studio Palterer, Florence, Italy.

# DeLight

DeLight, a 20 watt halogen lamp suspended between a pair of telescoping arms, projects light onto a whitelight reflection hologram of a glowing light that stares back from the base. The lamp, a parody of itself, was designed by Stiletto Studios, Berlin, West Germany, and is produced by Lank Kommunikation, Cologne-Pulheim, West Germany.

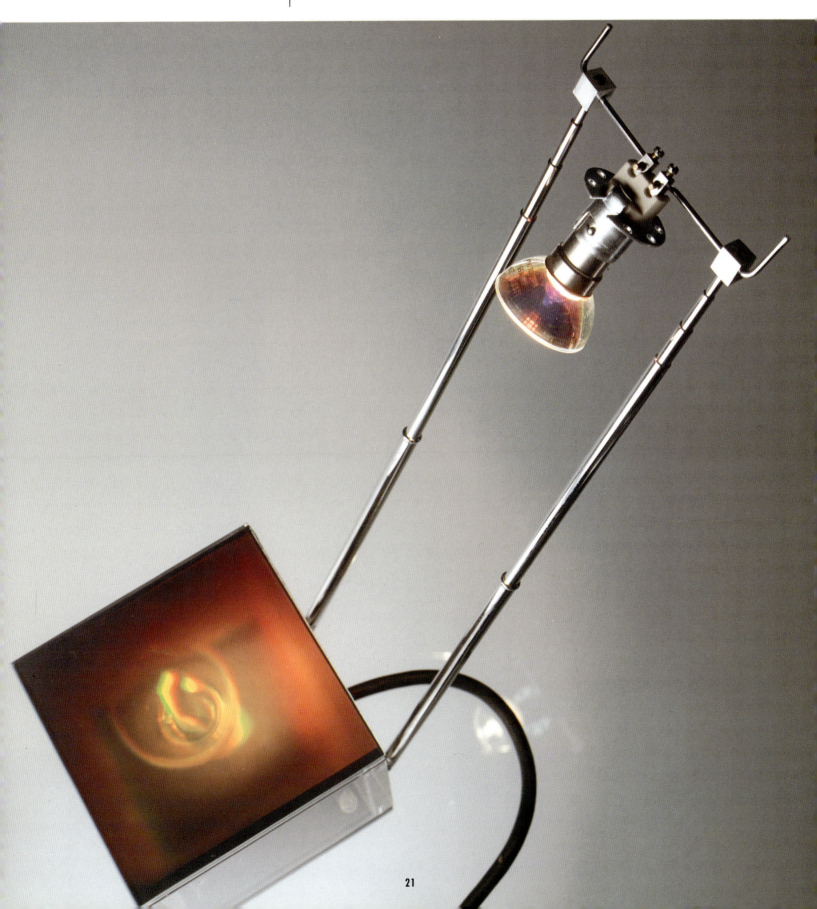

**1987-1989**
Luminous Chair: Length 650mm x Width 500mm x Height 850mm;
Sail: Length 400mm x Width 400mm x Height 1520mm;
Nest: Length 400mm x Width 400mm x Height 1460mm

These three lamps, designed and fabricated by Kyrre Andersen of Trikk, Oslo, Norway, experiment with the diffusion of light through different mediums. Luminous Chair houses a fluorescent tube inside its seat that illuminates the chair's polycarbonate slatted body; Sail's PVC sheeting is lit by a halogen bulb shining up from its steel base; and Nest is a wiry mass of cooper colored steel, cast alight by a halogen bulb set in its base.

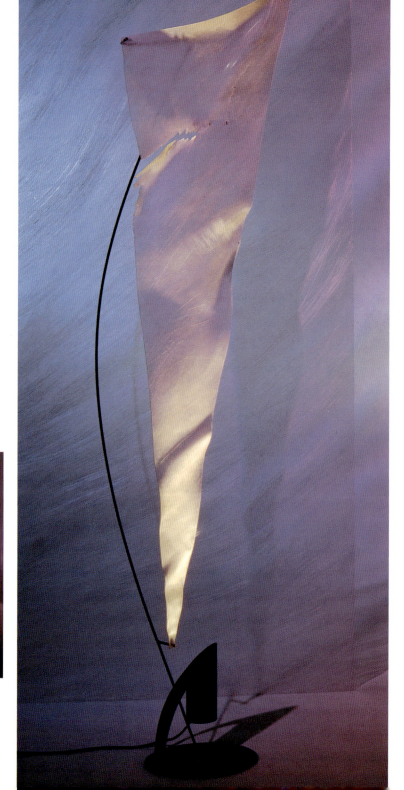

## Luna Pendant

**1986**
**Height 24in, 30in, 36in, or 42in x Diameter 18in**

With a glass disc and two quarter sphere chrome-plated pockets that house the halogen light source, Luna Pendant is a solid unit that rotates 360 degrees. Suspended by black vinyl-coated suspension cable from a transformer housed in the canopy, the Luna Pendant was designed Kevin Von Kluck for Boyd Lighting, San Francisco, California.

# Moon Tower

**1987**
**Height 32in x Width 21in x Depth 6in**

Weighing over 75 pounds, this massive table lamp is made of cast bronze; its sharp

pyramidal spire cuts into a sheet of 3/4 inch sand-etched, semi-circular glass.

Moontower was designed by Paul Ruine of Ruine Design Associates, Inc., New York.

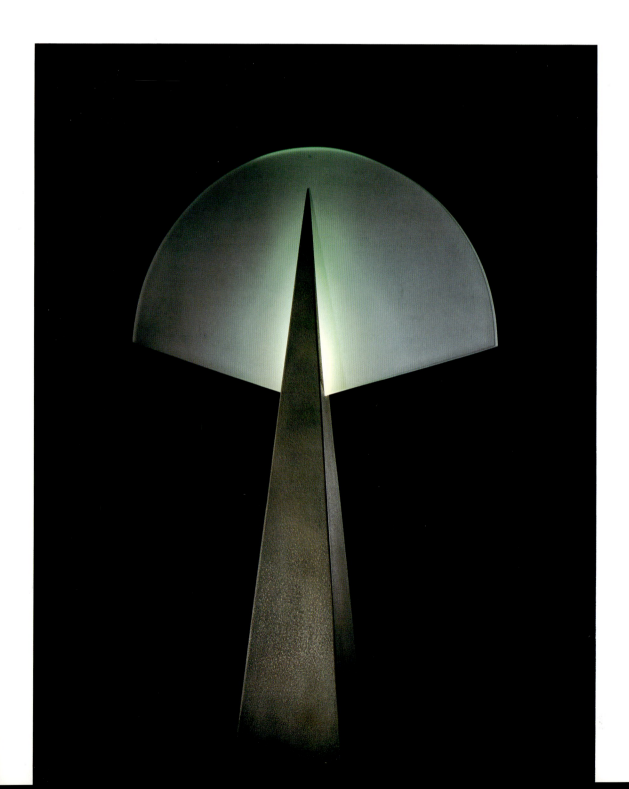

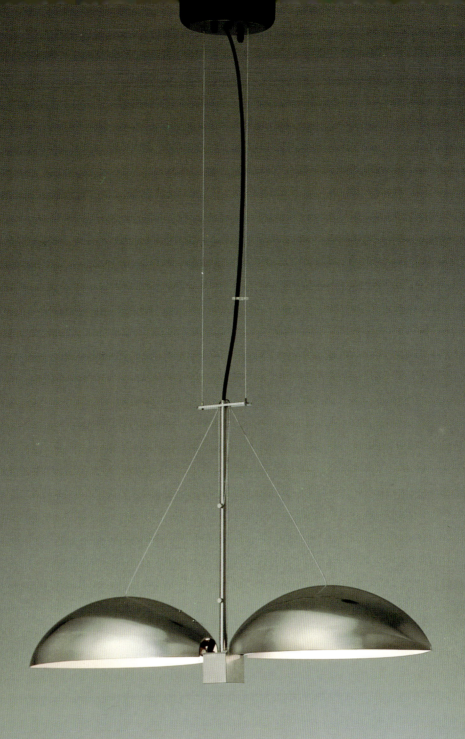

## Swag Lamp

**1987**

Swag is fabricated from a pair of highly polished metal domes joined together by a small metal box that houses a transformer. Looking like two heavy-lidded eyes, the lamp, suspended from the ceiling by tension cables, was designed and produced by Sinya Okayama, Osaka, Japan. Swag is distributed in the United States by Gallery 91, New York.

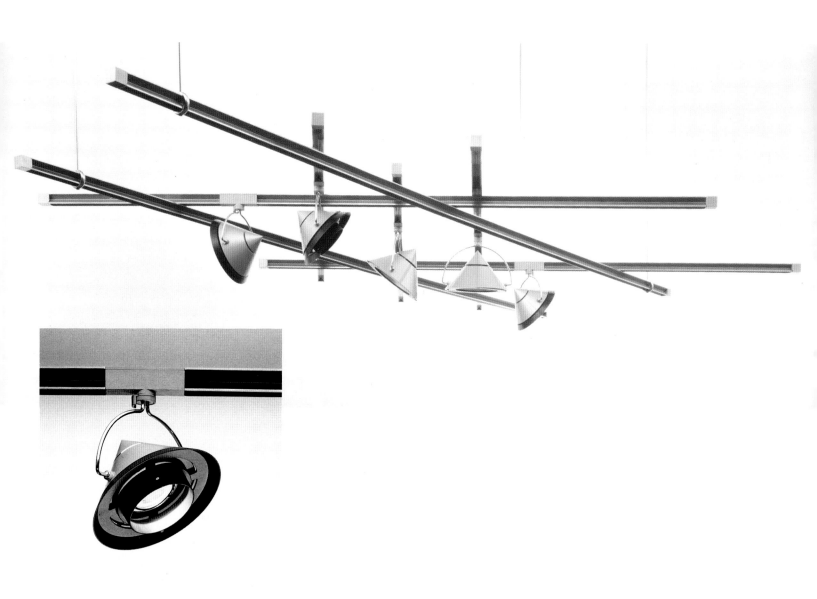

| *Mikado* | |
|---|---|
| **1989** | A low-voltage track lighting system, Mikado is made up of die-cast, cone-shaped spotlights supported by extruded anodized aluminum conductor profiles suspended by rods from the ceiling or wall. The pieces assemble in a number of ways, either for specific task and exhibition display lighting, or for large interior spaces where they can be hung at different levels symmetrically or asymmetrically. Mikado was designed by Ferdinand A. Porsche, Zell em See, Austria, and produced by Artemide Litech, Long Island City, New York. |

# *Verte A and Verte P*

**1987**
**Verte A: Height 190mm x Length 320mm;**
**Verte P: Diameter 340mm x Length 320mm;**

Verte A, a wall sconce, and Verte P, a ceiling lamp, both use minimal means to create a soft glow of light. Verte A has a brushed aluminum base from which its tempered glass diffuser hinges to spread light against the wall. Verte P works on the same principal but uses two sheets of tempered glass, hinged at the center, to diffuse and direct light. The lamps are manufactured by Metalarte, Barcelona, Spain, and were designed in-house by Sergi Devesa.

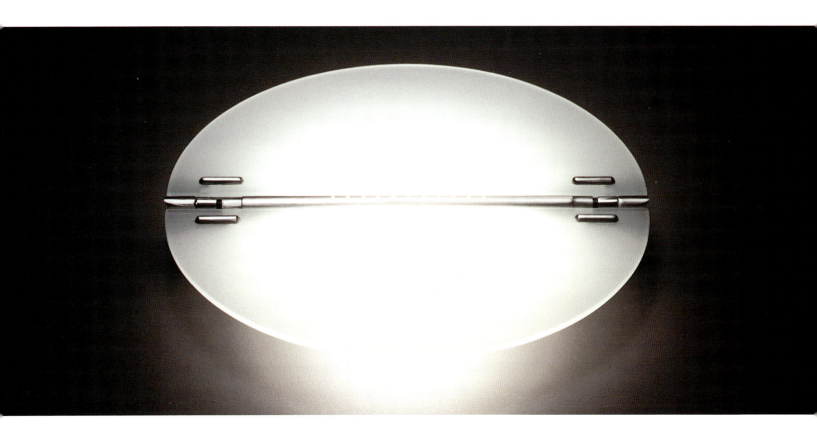

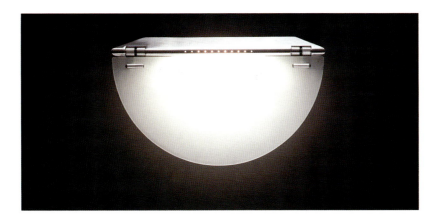

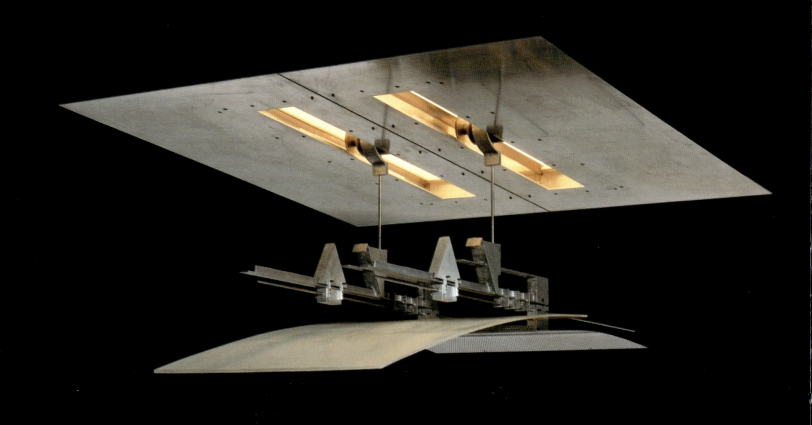

## Balisk

1987

This industrial looking light was designed by Morphosis, Santa Monica, California, and manufactured by Yamagiwa Co. Ltd., Tokyo, Japan. The lamp is mounted to the ceiling by a slotted aluminum top plate that houses the incandescent light source. The rest of the fixture hangs from an assortment of steel mechanisms and slides the distance of the two light insets. The aluminum panels suspended below cut and disperse the light.

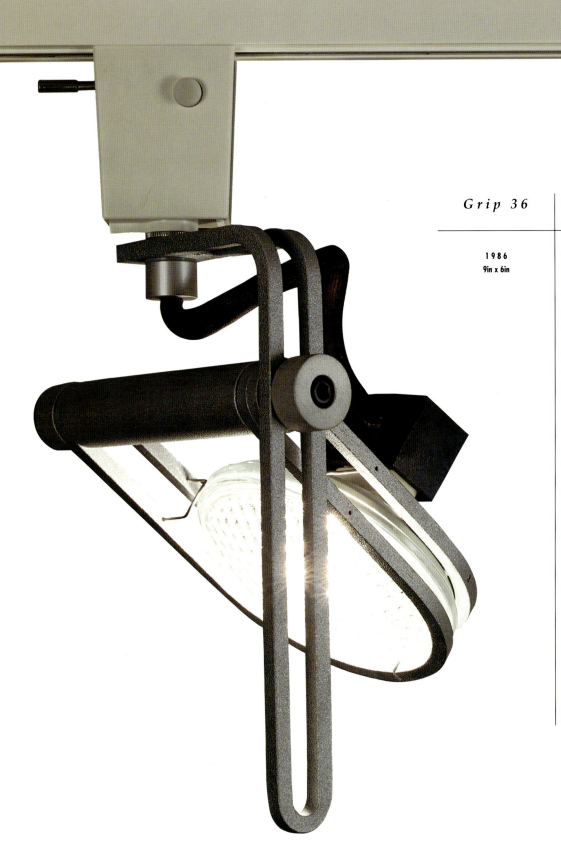

## Grip 36

**1986**
**9in x 6in**

Designed by Gary Payne of Magnan Payne Associates, New York, and manufactured by Lazin Lighting, New York, Grip 36 is both a wall sconce and track fixture. The lamp adjusts along the length of its support arm, and in the case of the track fixture, an additional mechanism rotates the lamp head 360 degrees. Both versions are made of powder-coated or anodized cast aluminum.

## Lashtal Sconce

**1988**
**20in x 12in x 5in**

Like a prop designed for the medieval stage, the Lashtal Sconce has a chain-mail shroud diffusing and reflecting the halogen light that shines from behind. The lamp was designed and produced by John Beckman and Pouran Esrefily of Axis Mundi, New York.

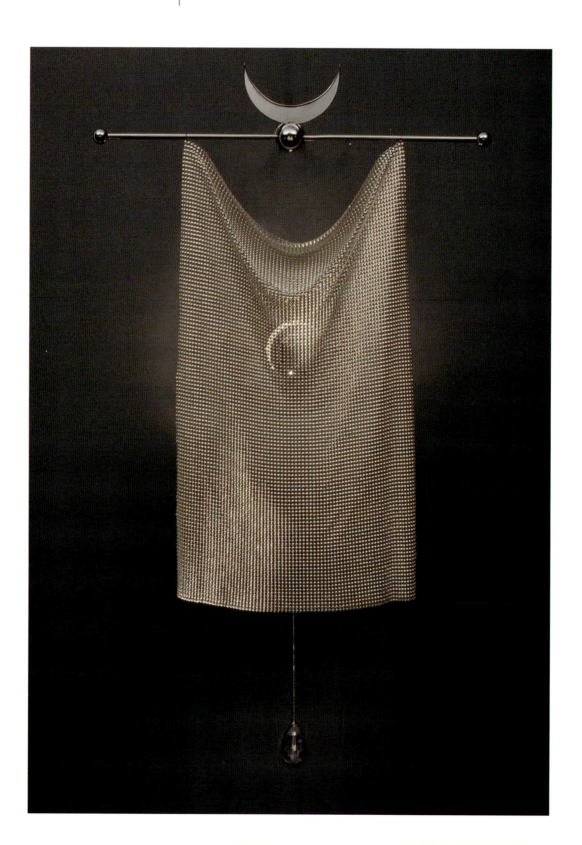

**1987**
Table lamp: 25in x 21in; Ceiling lamp: 25in x 67in; Shade Diameter 22in

Floating on chrome-plated supports, the elegant ellipsoidal Frankfurt lamps were designed by Pep Sant and Ramon Bigas of Associate Designer, S.A., Barcelona, Spain, for Belux. Either suspended from the ceiling by cables or mounted on a cast steel base, both versions of the lamp rotate 360 degrees on their axis

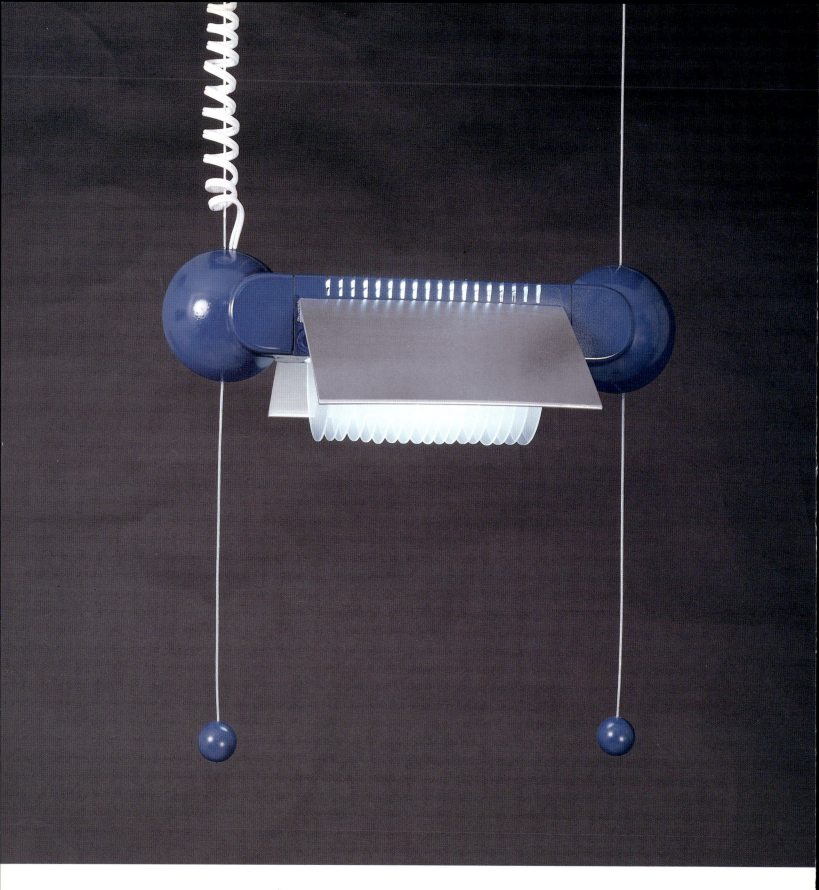

*Serena*

**1986**
**13in x 5in x 9in**

Designed and produced by Robert Wendrich of Mobius Design, Montreal, Canada, Serena is a lively ceiling light that makes use of color and playful forms. Suspended by two cables with a distinctive blue ball at each end, the lamp is made of coated metal and polyacetale discs that help diffuse the fluorescent light.

*Flut*

**1987**

Designed in-house by Erio Bosi for F.lli Martini S.p.A., Concordia, Italy, Flut is a highly flexible modular lighting system made of a collection of adjustable light fittings that simply plug into a central tube.

## Tata

**1988**
5in x 1 1/2in x 2 1/2in

Tata is a miniature rechargeable emergency light; its connecting plug conveniently rotates and tucks away behind a moveable panel. This hand-sized light, made of polycarbonate, was designed by Eros Bollani of Eros Bollani Design, Modena, Italy, for G.P.B. Begelli srl, Bologna, Italy.

## Pocket Lamp

**1987**
104mm x 48mm x 18mm

This practical pocket-size torch is activated by sliding down the top cover. Marketed for children, the lamp comes in playful bright colors or in black, and can be worn dangling around the neck. The Pocket Lamp was designed in-house by Robert Blaich and Judith Van Brunschot of Philips Lighting, Eindhoven, The Netherlands.

**1986**
1¹/₄in x ³/₄in x Length 4in

Simply an elliptical cylinder cut at 45 degrees, the Polyphemus flashlight rotates to any angle. The flashlight was designed by Emilio Ambasz, New York, for G.B. Plast, Bergamo, Italy.

### Comoda

**1987**

Based on the generic utility work light but with some added practical features, this portable and wireless torch has a rechargeable base and useful hook. Made of poly-carbonate, Comoda was designed by Eros Bollani of Eros Bollani Design, Modena, Italy, for G.P.B. Begelli srl, Bologna, Italy.

*Dea*

by Studio De Pas,
D'Urbino and Lomazzi

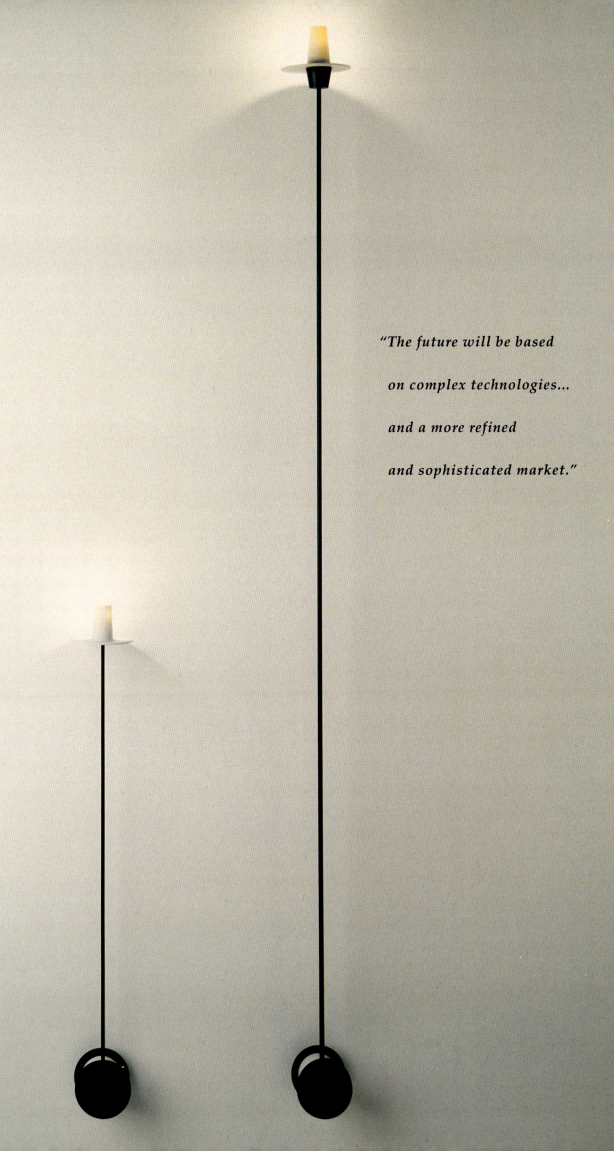

*"The future will be based*

*on complex technologies...*

*and a more refined*

*and sophisticated market."*

BORDO IN
GOMMA

SEZIONE
PIANTA

ø 111

FRONTE

FIANCO

JACK

INTERRUTTORE
CON DIMMER

DISCHETTI IN
POLIURETANO
INTEGRALE

## *Dea*

**1987**
Length 110mm x Width 90mm x Height 830mm or 1770mm

Designed by Studio De Pas D'Urbino Lomazzi in Milan, Italy, Dea is a halogen sconce attached to the wall by a special jack housed within its spool-shaped base. A long slender aluminum tube projects upwards from the base, delicately supporting a candle-like ceramic diffuser. Based on the small metal lamps that illuminate some tooling machines, Dea's minimal and elongated style suggests pure elegance. Dea is part of the Zeus Collection manufactured by Noto SRL, also of Milan.

# Interview

*In 1966, Jonathan De Pas, Donato D'Urbino and Paolo Lomazzi opened their industrial design and architecture studio in Milan. During the sixties, they developed a specific interest in furniture and temporary architecture, designing a series of pneumatic structures for the Italian Pavilion at the Osaka World Expostion and for the 14th Triennale of Milan. With a prolific output in furniture design, their clients have included Acerbis, Artemide, BBB, Driade, Poltronova, Sirrah and Zanotta. Their designs are part of the permanent collections of the Museum of Modern Art in New York, the Victoria and Albert Museum in London and the Pompidou Center in Paris, among others.*

**How were you influenced or inspired?** Very casually one day, while looking in an ironmonger's shop, we found a little lamp (see sketch) used for tool machines like lathes and sewing machines. **Did you use any special materials or technology?** Wall lamps require current inlet at the connection point of the lamp, but Dea has to be introduced directly into existing current taps without requiring any modification of the electrical installation. Therefore, we developed a three-jack connection system for use in Europe, Germany and the United States. **What was the biggest obstacle?** The electric installation regulations of different countries are not unified. We had to work around this problem. **What alternatives were explored?** We explored assembling different jack connections on the body of one lamp. **What would you like to design next?** We are working on lamps using industrially treated ceramics and blown glass. **What is the future of lighting design?** There will be two trends. The first will be based on complex technologies produced in strict cooperation between the designers and engineers of lighting companies. The other will be more refined and sophisticated and will address the needs of a rich and demanding market.

## Dynamite

Made of neoprene rubber, this playful yet sinister looking table lamp was designed to resemble the charge box of a dynamite bomb. Created by Jan van Opzeeland of Dutch Design, Finsterwolde, The Netherlands, Dynamite is distributed by Gallery 91, New York.

**1988**
6in x 6in x 24in

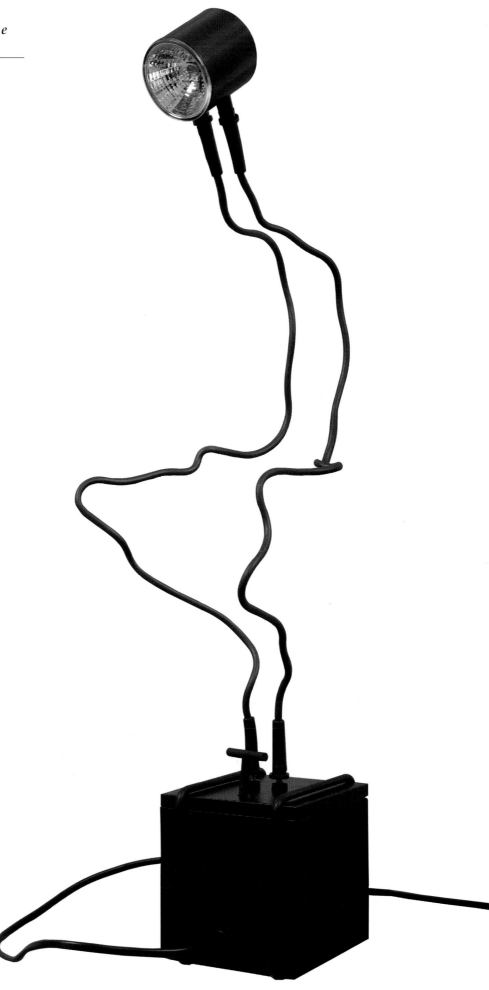

42

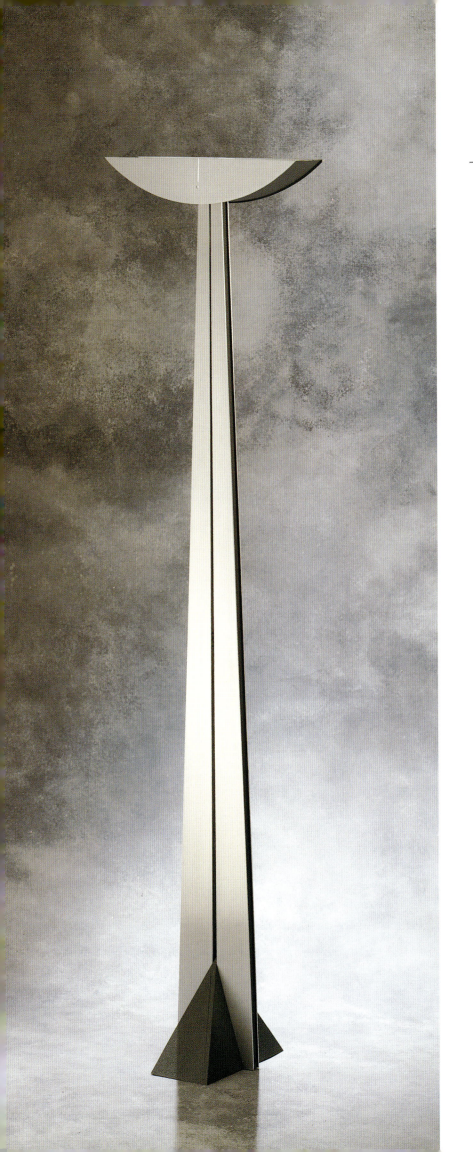

## Motto Yubi Torchiere

**1988**
**Height 69 in; Shade 18in x 4in; Base 10in x 6in**

A noble monument to Japanese architecture, Motto Yubi is a halogen torchiere fabricated from satin aluminum. The lamp was designed by Robert Sonneman of Sonneman Design Group Inc., Long Island City, New York, for George Kovacs Lighting Inc., New York.

## Iló-Ilú

**1987**
**Cable length 1400mm -1900mm**

Like a circus trapeze act, the two versions of Iló-Ilú consist of an assemblage of minia-

ture objects, mirrors, spheres, arrows and tiny halogen bulbs, balancing together on

wire cables suspended from the ceiling. The first version has a blue spherical coun-

terweight, an adjustable arrow and a mirror that reflects light from the halogen bulb;

adjusting any one of these elements re-directs the light. The other, more austere ver-

sion has a simple black counterweight; its reflector points downwards providing

direct light. Iló-Ilú was designed and produced by Ingo Maurer and team, Design M

Ingo Maurer GmbH, Munich, West Germany.

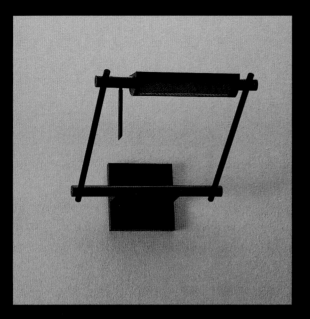

**1987**
Sconce: Length 14in; Floor lamp:
Height 75in; Task lamp: Height 35in
x Extension 35in

Sleek and minimal, the three versions of Logo—a sconce, task and floor lamp—are all made of black anodized aluminum and have steel mesh diffusers. Their support structures and mechanisms, however, are quite different. The floor lamp stands on two parallel legs while its cylindrical shade rotates on its axis. The sconce pivots from its base attached to the wall; the task lamp stands on a tubular leg, with its diffuser balanced by a counterweight. Logo was designed in-house by Mario Barbaglia and Marco Colombo, Paf, Milan, Italy, and distributed in the United States by Koch and Lowy Inc., Long Island City, New York.

## *Maya*

**1987**
**18in x 54in**

Fabricated from fan-folded paper, one of the most traditional and effective methods of diffusing light, Maya is a floor or desk lamp designed and produced by Daniel T. Ebihara of Gallery 91, New York. Maya also folds into a compact package for shipping.

*Argo*

**1988**
**Track lengths of 20in, 39in, 79in and 118in**

Designed by Richard Sapper, Milan, Italy, Argo is a low voltage track lighting system made of extruded and die-cast aluminum. A sleek extension to the spotlight housing allows the light to be rotated 360 degrees: in addition, the spotlight is equipped with an integrated track adaptor, making it easily positioned anywhere on the track. Argo is manufactured by Artemide, Inc., Long Island City, New York.

## Café Olé

Designed by Christian Theill, Florence, Italy, this graceful halogen floor lamp features a gentle peach-like diffuser, made of translucent ceramics, positioned on top of a 1.6 meter long tubular support. Refined yet playful, Café Olé is part of the Zeus Collection manufactured by Noto SRL, Milan, Italy.

**1986**
**Diameter 220mm x Height 1660mm**

## Lyra

**1987**
**Max height 3500mm**

With four adjustable and swivelling halogen lamps suspended between vertical parallel wires, Lyra was designed by Giuseppe Raimondi for Light Solutions East, New York.

## Satelight

**1986**
**Diameter 4450mm**

Satelight, designed and manufactured by Stiletto Studios, Berlin, West Germany, is a far from ordinary table light. The lamp's tubular incandescent light source is contained within a stainless steel washing machine drum supported by three legs. A glass top transforms the lamp into a night table; its built-in light glows and reflects off the polished surface of the drum.

*Heron*

1989

An adjustable halogen table lamp, the sophisticated and sober Heron is made of black lacquered metal. Perched on a shiny wire frame, the lamp swings back and forward to provide indirect or task lighting. Heron was designed by Samuel Ribet for Stilnovo, Milan, Italy.

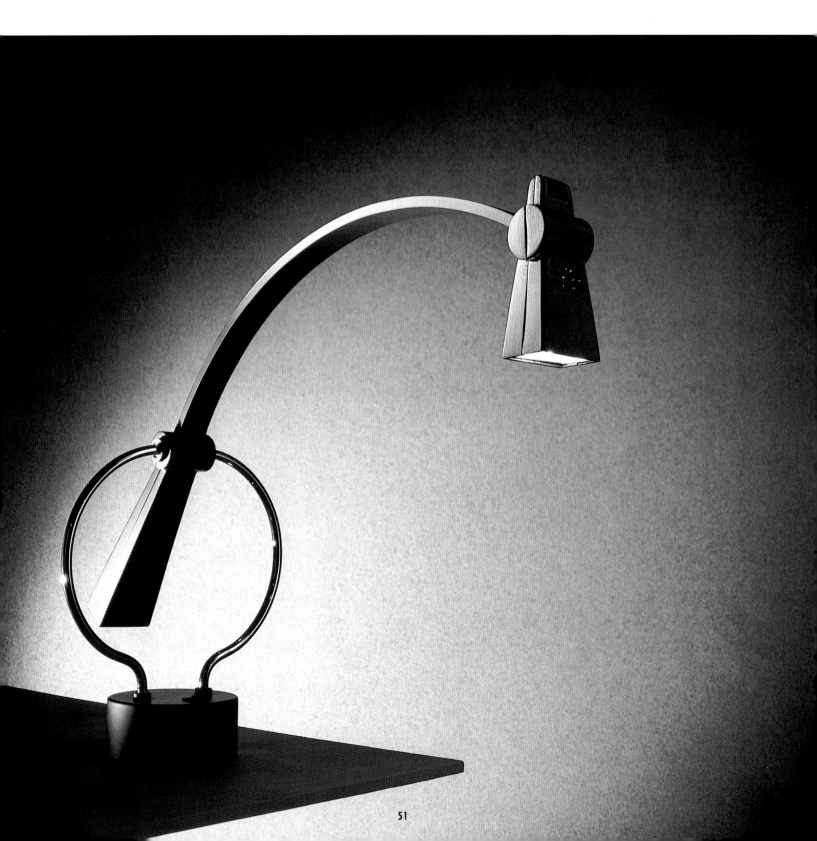

paint. The lamp is part of the Zeus Collection manufactured by Noto SRL, Milan,

Italy, and was designed by Maurizio Peregali of Noto.

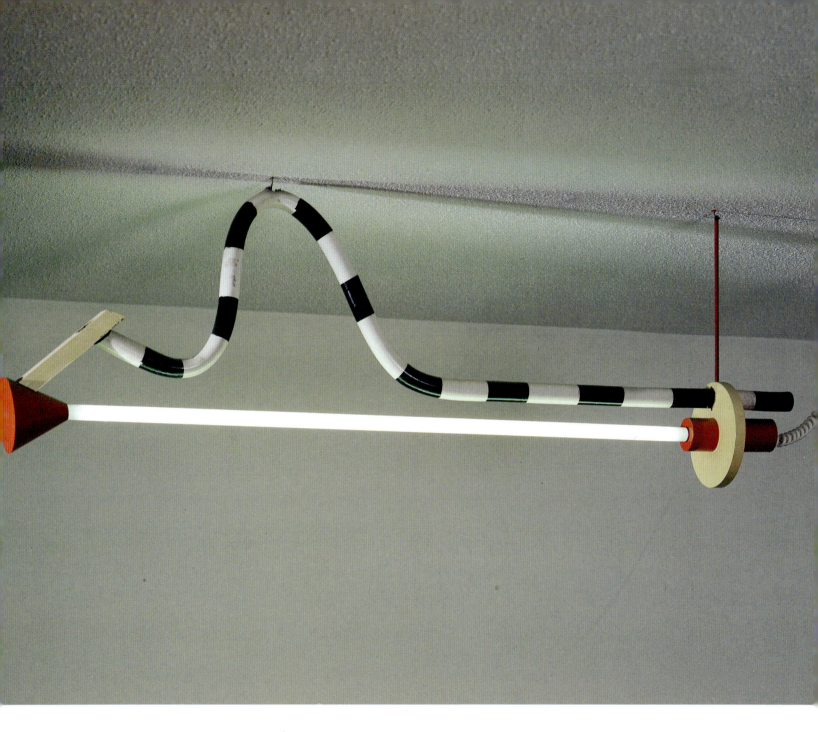

## Serpentina

**1987**
**Height 500mm x Width 185mm x Length 11500mm**

This light fixture makes playful use of the industrial fluorescent tube. Designed by Johanne Peter Klien of Design Form Technik AG, Liechtenstein, Serpentina hangs from the ceiling like a curvy snake. Painted with black and white stripes, the lamp hangs horizontally, suspended by cables from the ceiling, over an exposed fluorescent tube.

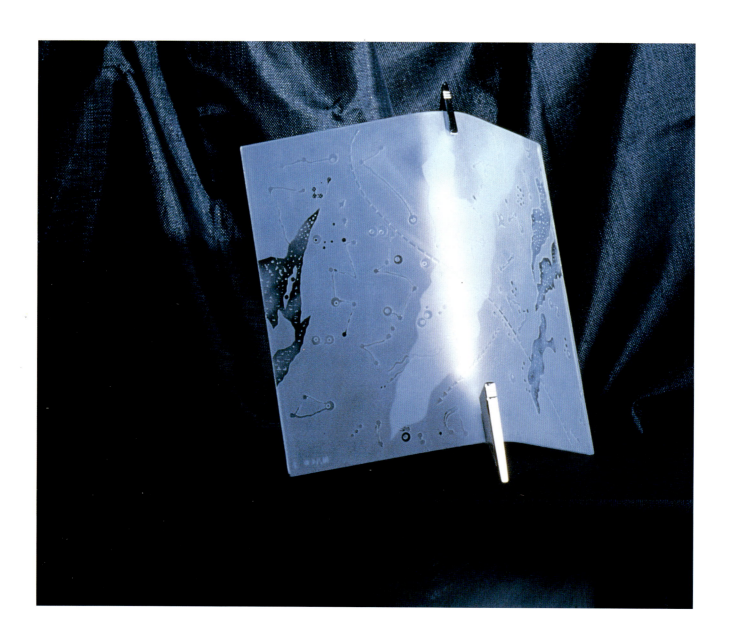

*Antinous*

1986
440mm x 420mm x 230mm

Made of sandblasted sheet glass held in place by a fine nickled-steel leg, Antinous, an incandescent desk lamp, is formed to look like an open book, one that "protects the reader," say the designers. The pattern engraved in the glass represents an imaginary dream galaxy. Antinous was designed by Studio Naço, Paris, France, and produced by K.L. Diffusion, also of Paris.

## Plana

**Floor lamp: Height 78in;
Sconce: 9.5in x 10in**

With blown acidified glass diffusers which are available in translucent blue or white, the Plana halogen sconce and floor lamps were designed by Carlo Urbanati Ricci of Tech Lighting, Chicago, for Foscarini, Murano, Italy.

*City View Lighthouses*

1984

An expansive landscape of twinkling lights, City View was designed and produced by James Evanson, New York. This collection of unique fixtures, each housing an incandescent globe, invites the audience to interact with the design. Each lamp is make of laquered fiber board; the subtle city colors are created from moveable pieces of plexiglass that can be repositioned in and around the lamps. Together or separately, these lamps create a distinctive mood.

**1989**
16in x 72in; 16in x 60in;
11in x 24in

Designed by Red Square, New York, for Gallery 91, New York, Transform floor lamps are made of white translucent acrylic shapes that can be assembled in various configurations. Hand painted incandescent light bulbs create a haze of brilliant color through the plastic.

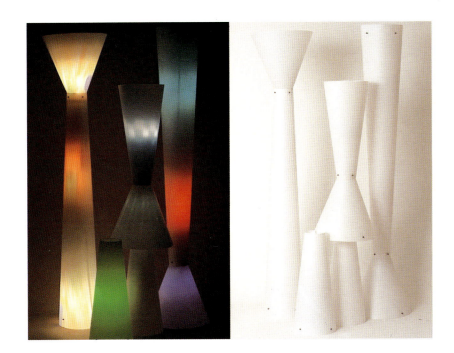

**1989**
16in x 72in; 16in x 60in;
11in x 24in

# Illuminated Magnifier

by Human Factors
Industrial Design

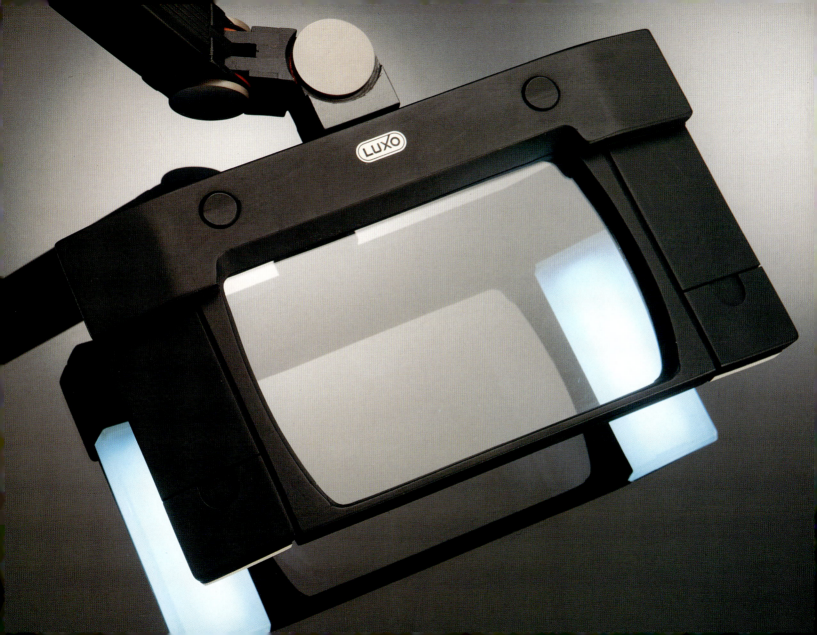

FLEX JOINT
(ALL AXES)

(COUNTERWEIGHTS

SWIVEL

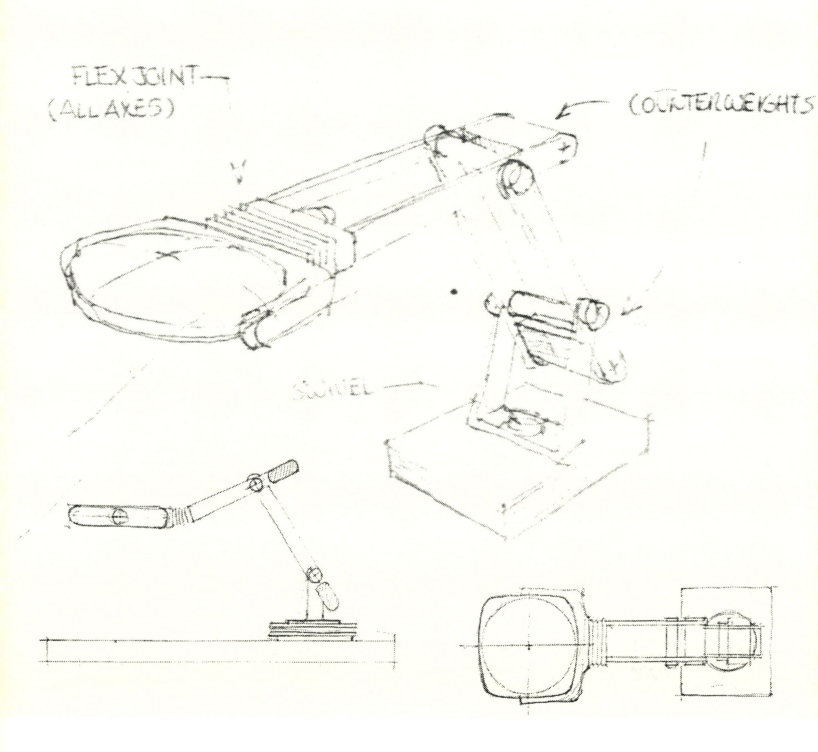

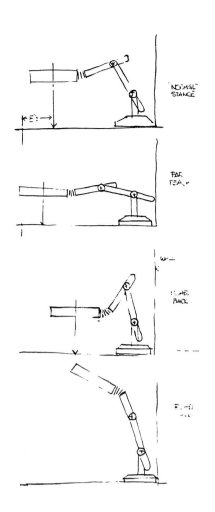

## Illuminated Magnifier

**1985**
Lens: 6 1/4in x 4 1/2in; Arm: 31in

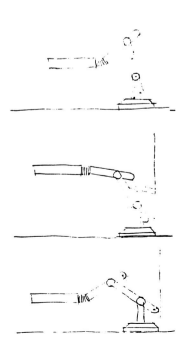

After extensive research involving task analysis and definition of user require-ments, Douglas Spranger, Paul Mulhauser and Mark Steiner of Human Factors Industrial Design, New York, developed an illuminated magnifier to suit the specific needs of circuit board inspectors, artists and engineers. With an enlarged rectangular viewing area, the magnifier has a 7-watt fluorescent lamp on either side of the lens to provide balanced illumination or side lighting. Replacing conventional round magnifiers that house integral flourescent lamps, the magnifier is mage of metal and shrouded in molded plastic. Attached to an adjustable arm, the lamp moves smoothly over the work surface it has to magnify. The Illuminated Magnifier is manufactured by Luxo Lamp Corporation, Port Chester, New York.

# Interview

*Douglas M. Spranger (middle) is president of Human Factors Industrial Design Inc., a design firm that he founded in 1974. The recipient of a masters degree in industrial design from the Pratt Institute in 1972, Spranger is listed as the co-inventor on twenty-two patents, including the design of several patient care devices and surgical instruments. Paul Mulhauser (right), vice-president of Human Factors Industrial Design, graduated from the Pratt Institute in 1974. His work includes shipboard electronic navigation equipment and small desktop-mounted terminals. Mark Steiner (left), senior design affiliate of the firm, graduated in 1982 from Syracuse University. In 1989, Steiner established his own design consultancy in New York, where he supports Human Factors Industrial Design in-house programs on a continuing basis.*

**How was the project initiated?**   Luxo Lamp Corporation wanted to develop an illuminated magnifier for electronic circuit board inspection tasks. We were contracted to study specific user needs and to develop a large field-of-view lens with appropriate lighting.   **How were you influenced or inspired?**   For decades, the desk magnifier of choice for artists, engineers and parts inspectors has been a round magnifier with an integral fluorescent lamp attached to an adjustable arm. With the explosion of electronic printed circuit boards and the need for minute inspection, Luxo wisely identified new needs—a larger rectangular field of view consistent with PCB formats and appropriate illumination for low-profile or surface inspection.   **Did you use any special materials or technology?**   We developed a new magnifier head which provides a thirteen-inch horizontal field-of-view, a fifty-three percent increase over convential round magnifers. Two individually controlled 7-watt flourescent lamps are integrated into the lamp head to provide either balanced illumination or side lighting, which effectively highlights surface imperfections.   **What was the biggest obstacle?**   Sizing the large glass lens at a reasonable weight, providing adequate illumination with two standard PC-7 flourescent tubes and conceiving a "next generation" adjustable arm.   **Evaluate the success of your design.**   Given the lamp's small market niche and the fact that it meets a very specific need, we consider this design solution quite succesful.   **What would you like to design next?**   We would like to develop two lighting products. One, an eyebrow-style accessory lamp for CRT based consoles—a very real need exists for providing flexible worksurface lighting. The other, a lightweight, self-contained, head mounted lamp for surgeons.   **What is the future of lighting design?**   Functional, low cost lighting for specific applications will emerge. Workplaces are filled with CRTs and only crude provisions are made to prevent screen reflection. Therefore, specialized lighting will replace conventional 2 x 4 fluorescent and under-counter task lights.

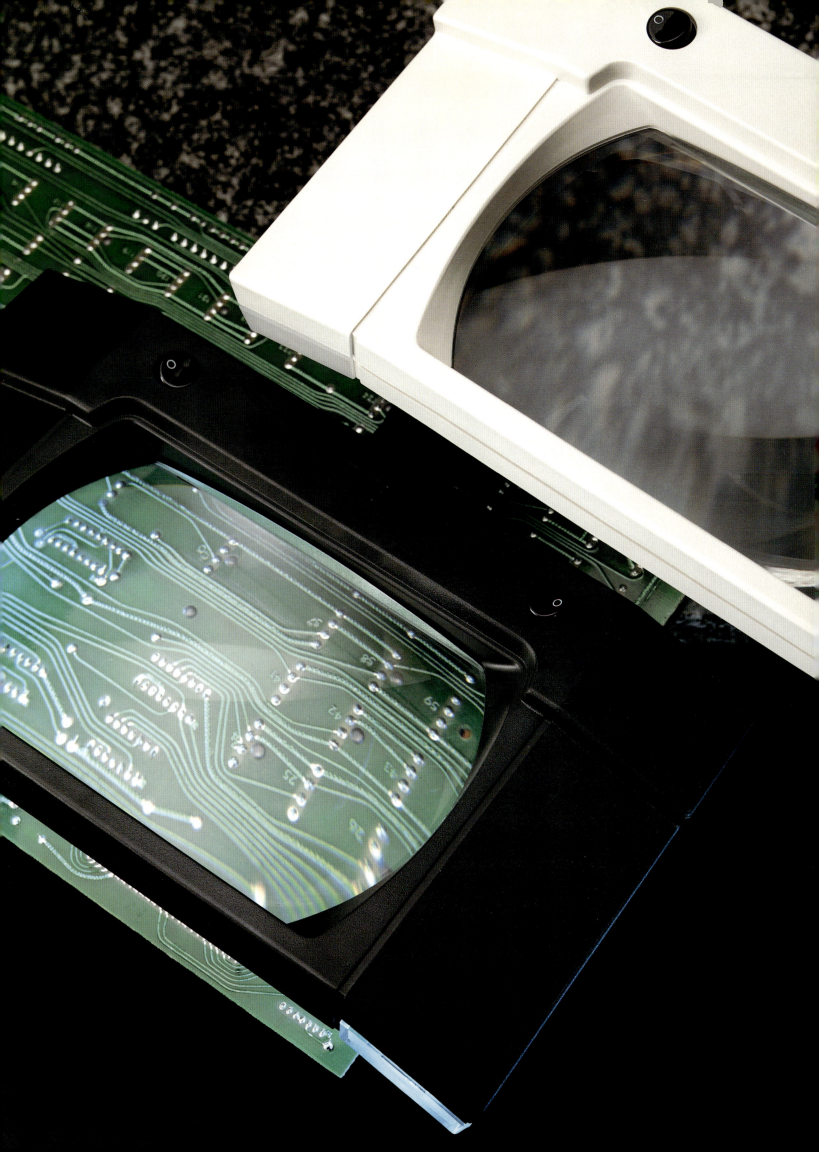

## *Ara*

**1 9 8 8**
**Base diameter 7in x Height 22in**

Made of polished chrome-plated steel, this pixie-like halogen table lamp was designed by Philippe Starck, Montfort L'Amaury, France, and manufactured by Flos S.p.A., Brescia, Italy. The lamp is powered by tilting the horn-shaped lamphead up or down.

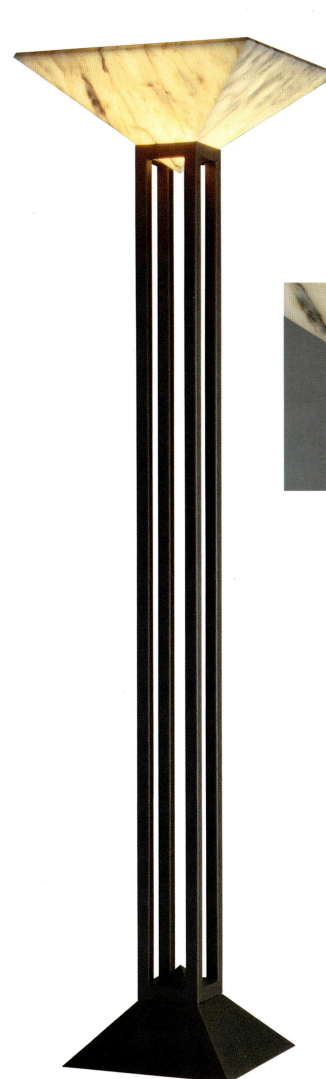

## *Piramide Lamp*

**1988**
**72in high**

Classical forms join in harmonious union to create this six-foot floor lamp by Marco Pasanella, Pasanella Furniture, New York. A black sandblasted steel column rises from a pyramidal steel base to support a second pyramid —this one inverted and made of translucent alabaster—housing the halogen light source.

## Winged Victory

**1988**
**Height 72in x Width 17in x Depth 12in**

This wall-floor lamp leans effortlessly away from the wall and into the room, support-

ed by two fine wires. With triangular stamped sheet metal wings riveted to a six-foot-

long metal tube, the lamp comes in either a zinc, ferrous or verdigris finish. Winged

Victory was designed in-house by David Baird of Ziggurat, La Jolla, California.

## *Fenix*

**Ceiling lamp: 500mm x 600mm; Floor lamp: 2000mm x 400mm**

Delicately suspended from the ceiling by fine wires or supported from the floor by a black metal structure, the Fenix lamps were designed and produced by Jorge A. Garcia Garay of Garcia Garay S.A. in Barcelona, Spain. Both the ceiling and floor lamp support graceful white aluminum wings that gently reflect light generated by a halogen bulb housed within a metal tube.

## Karl and Freddy

**1989**
Karl: 5in x 12 ½in x 67in ; Freddy:10in x 71in x 6in

Originally custom designed for Gianni Versace's New York showroom as a display light fixture, the Karl and Freddy lamps are designed and produced for limited production by Red Square, New York. Karl is a suspended ceiling lamp and his counterpart, Freddy, is a floor lamp. Both lamps are made of brass with a stainless steel surface treatment; their simply formed shades are made of sandblasted glass.

**1989**
**Floor lamp: Height 72in x Width
10in; Table lamp: Height 22 3/4in
x Width 10in**

Designed by Jorge Pensi of Artup Lighting, Santa Ana, California, Regina is a low voltage table or floor lamp with a polished cast aluminum base and shade. The shade slides up and down on stainless steel supports that conduct power to the halogen bulb.

## Tikal

**1985**
Width 19in x Height 17.7in

Made of polished and sand blasted glass, injection molded methacrylate, aluminum and zinc alloy, Tikal incorporates two translucent diffusers, one opal white and one grey, to create different intensities of light. This incandescent table lamp was designed by P.G. Ramella for Atelier International Lighting, Long Island City, New York.

## Elroy

**1988**

Combining a paper shade, handmade from the Japanese kozo and gampi plants, with a turned wood column and onyx base, Liz Galbraith of Philadelphia, Pennsylvania, has created an elegantly styled table lamp. The organic shapes, soft textures and natural translucency of the materials used were inspired by the work of Isamu Noguchi and the Shakers.

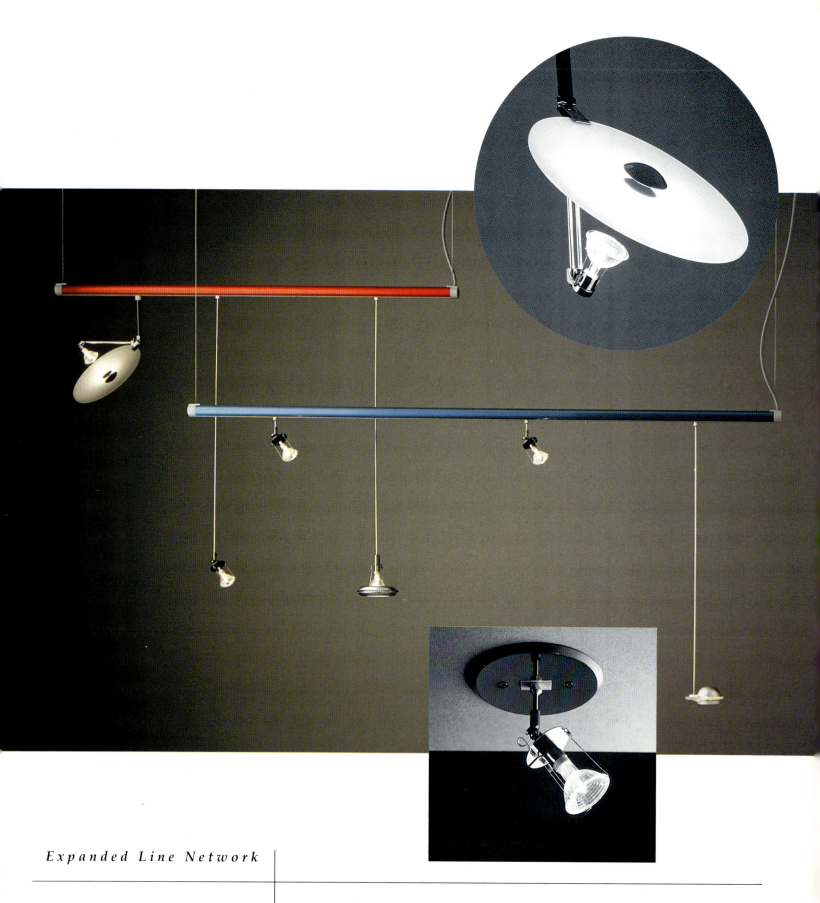

## Expanded Line Network

**1988**
Track: 52in or 71in; Fixture rods: 20in or 30in

This versatile line of track lighting, which incorporates four interchangeable and distinctive halogen fixture heads, was designed by Perry King and Santiago Miranda of King Miranda Associates, Milan, Italy, for Flos Inc., Huntington Station, New York. Up to six halogen fixtures plug into the suspended anodized aluminum track, allowing the user to create a number of different configurations. Any of the four fixture heads can be used as individual ceiling or desk units.

## Lunatica

**1989**
**1750mm x 450mm x 300mm**

Designed by Donatella Costa

for Vistosi, Venice, Italy,

Lunatica is a floor lamp with

delightful multi-colored

Murano glass diffusers. The

blue, yellow and grey glass

discs can be swivelled,

spreading and mixing tones

of light.

# On-Off

**1989**
6½in x 5in

Fabricated from unbreakable and flexible polyurethane, the On-Off lamp derives its name from a simple counterweight in its base that allows the lamp to balance from side to side turning on or off in the process. Designed by Meda, Raggi and Santachiara for Artemide Inc., Long Island City, New York, the lamp comes in white, pink or blue.

**1988**
Height 80in x Width 24in x
Diameter 24in

Dramatic and mystical, this lamp, designed by Alex Locadia, New York, is named Shaman for the priest who uses magic to control ancestral spirits and demons. Tall and powerful, Shaman is made of blackened carved wood, steel, glass, gold leaf and horse hair; its halogen light source beams from behind a central gold disc, dispersing light across a larger disc of glass. The lamp is distributed by Art et Industrie, New York.

## *Altalena*

An elegantly poised low voltage table lamp, Altalena conducts energy from the transformers in its ABS base along aluminum arms to the halogen light source housed in a counter-balanced, ribbed Ryton shade. Altalena was designed by Pep Sant and Ramon Bigas of Associate Designers S.A., Barcelona, Spain, and manufactured by Luxo Italiana S.p.A., Presezzo, Italy.

**1984**
**Height 2050mm**

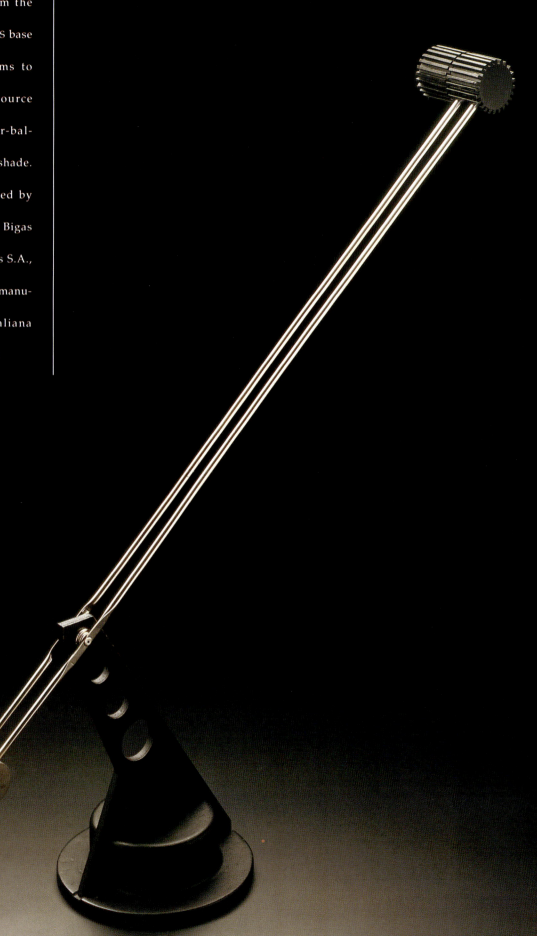

## Floor Lamp

1989
72in x 12in x 12in

With attention to fine detail and craftsmanship, this classic floor lamp was designed by Lee Weitzman of Lee Weitzman Studios, Chicago, Illinois. The lamp's base and support is elegantly constructed of mahogany, ebony and brass, while its shade is made of extremely thin sheets of birds-eye maple that become almost transparent when light shines through.

## A 2 6

**1988**
**Height 1800mm x Base Diameter 240mm**

Constructed from carbon fiber cloth, A26 is a towering floor lamp whose form reflects the construction techniques used in the aeronautics industry. Designed and produced by Miles Keller of Kerr Keller Design, Toronto, Canada, this bold halogen lamp transmits a tranquil, peaceful light.

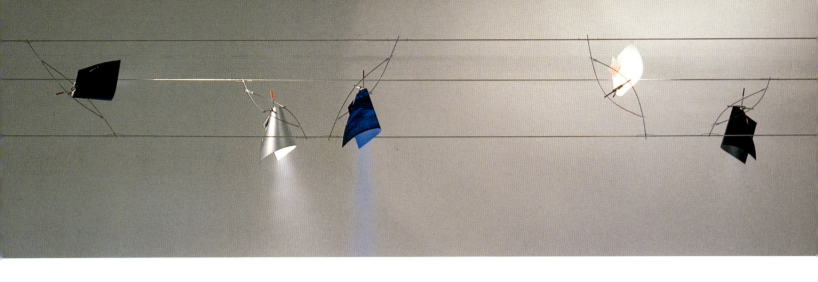

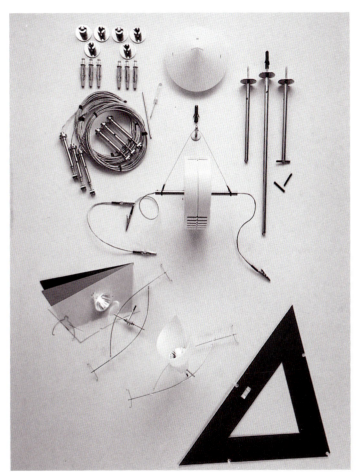

## BaKa-Rú

**1986**

BaKa-Rú is made up of a number of lighting elements, each housing a 50 watt halogen bulb. Perching like delicate birds on low-voltage wires, the elements, made of folded sheets of plastic, can be tilted, swivelled and repositioned; their parallel cable support is installed horizontally, vertically or at an angle. BaKa-Rú was designed and produced by Ingo Maurer and team of Design M Ingo Maurer GmbH, Munich, West Germany.

# Ruby Begonia

## by Alec Drummond

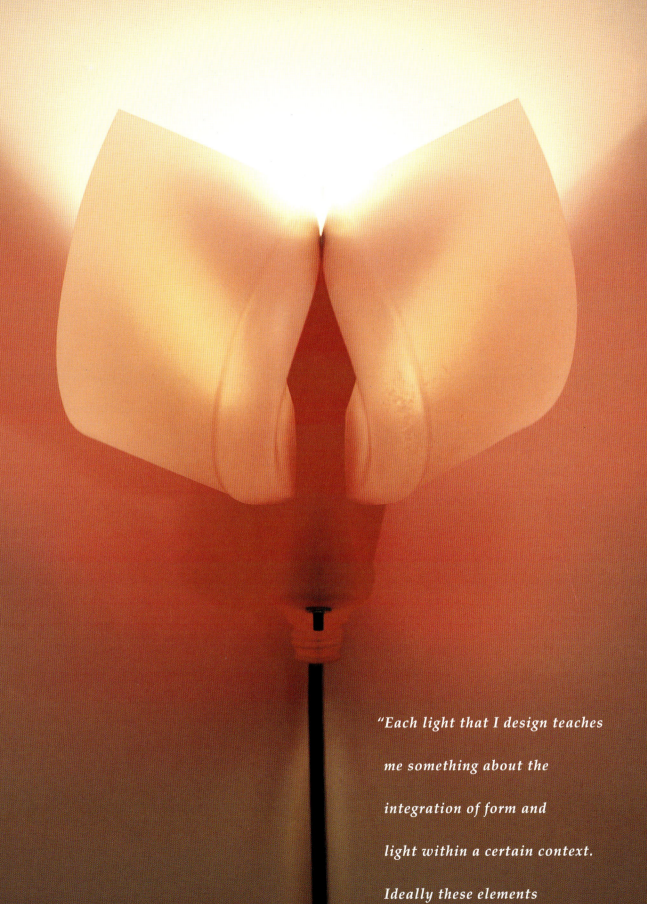

"Each light that I design teaches

me something about the

integration of form and

light within a certain context.

Ideally these elements

should become a whole using

the simplest terms."

## Ruby Begonia

**1988**
10in x 10in x 11in

Dramatic and voluptuous, Ruby Begonia is an incandescent wall sconce made of one of the cheapest and most plentiful of materials found in our throw-away society—plastic bottles. Reshaping and transforming the bottles and making clever use of the translucency and opacity of plastic, the designer, Alec Drummond of Brooklyn, New York, has created a unique and beautiful light out of what others might simply call trash. The sconce organically integrates its own shadow and at the same time casts rich tones of ruby red onto the wall.

# Interview

*Alec Drummond studied product and environmental design under Victor Papanek at Kansas City Art Institute, Missouri. After traveling and painting in Italy and in Spain, where he was inspired by Gaudi's direct use of indigenous forms and materials in architecture, Drummond returned to New York and became interested in experimental lighting using found objects and finished materials. In 1988 he started Shinola Lights in Brooklyn with glass artist Charles Flickinger in order to design lighting with environmentally sound materials and technologies. Drummond also works with the New Alchemy Institute in East Falmouth, Massaehussetts, to learn more about plant growth and ecological approaches to design.*

**How was the project initiated?**   The project was an inexpensive way of exploring organic form with light. I also wanted to get over the fear of using color and decoration since I don't believe simplicity has to be austere.   **How were you influenced or inspired?**   I was inspired by the economy and diversity found in the growth and form of plants.   **Did you use any special materials or technology?**   I consider plastic bottles a blight; however they make a very good raw material. They're easily manipulated and are unfortunately found everywhere.   **What was the biggest obstacle?**   The biggest obstacle was resisting the temptation to purchase a product just because of it plastic container and dump the contents down the drain.   **What alternatives were explored?**   Before I started designing with plastic bottles, I worked with paper, translating its form into sheet metal. For my purposes, this struck me as too wasteful of a natural resource.   **Evaluate the success of your design.**   Since the design is part of an on-going project, I don't consider any single light a success. Each light that I design teaches me something about the integration of form and light within a certain context. Ideally these elements should become a whole using the simplest means.   **What would you like to design next?**   I'd like to take what I've learned and design something more useful.   **What is the future of lighting design?**   I can't predict the future but I would like to see lighting designers use energy efficient lamps, materials and manufacturing—processes that don't weigh too heavily on the environment before or after they have become lights.

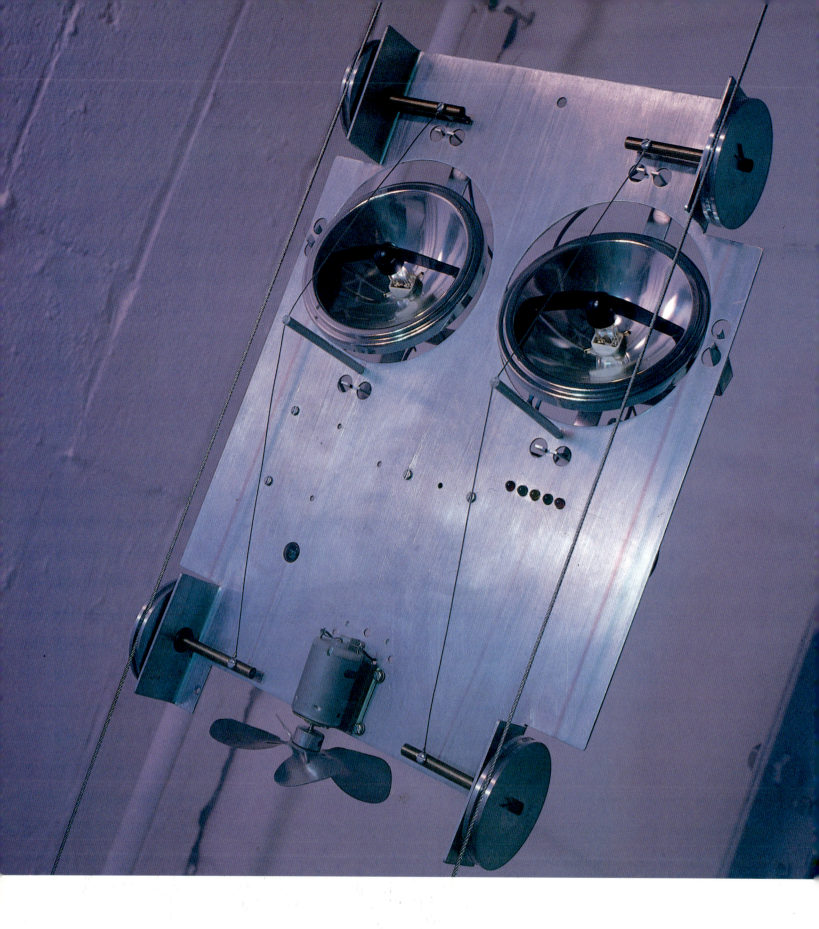

*Motorized Robotic Light*

**1 9 8 8**
250mm x 350mm x 100mm

Powered by a transformer, the Motorized Robotic Light travels across the ceiling on

a pair of conductive cables, collecting energy for its two halogen lamps as it moves.

Operated manually or by remote control, this computerized ceiling lamp was

designed and fabricated by Shiu-Kay Kan of SKK Lighting, London, England.

## Dede

**1989**
14in x 21½in

Made from blown white and aquamarine opaline glass and supported by a lacquered grey metal frame and solid base, this halogen table lamp was designed by Enzo Berti of VeArt, Venice, Italy and manufactured by Artemide Inc., Long Island City, New York.

### Zefiro

**1988**
Diameter 9in or 20in (depending on model) x Suspension height 96in

A series of hanging fixtures, Zefiro is made of two frosted glass components and is assembled with either a glass ring, an enamelled reflector or, as seen in this photograph, a sand-blasted glass diffuser. This incandescent ceiling lamp was designed by P.G. Ramella for Atelier International Lighting, Long Island City, New York.

## *Andrea*

**1987**
**Height 74in x Shade diameter 7in x Base 10in x 10in**

Sleek and classic, Andrea was created in-house at Koch + Lowy Inc., Long Island City,

New York, by Andrzej Duijas. The floor lamp is made of brass, chrome or painted

metal, and its halogen bulb creates a strong up-light for any space.

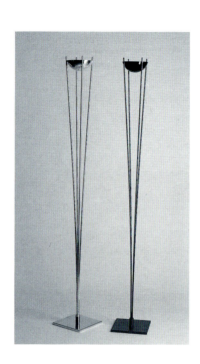

## Floor Lamp

**1989**
**Height: 56in; Shade 20in; Base 12in**

Designed and produced by Whitney Boin of Whitney Boin Studio, New York, this floor lamp combines unusual materials and form. Its steel and aluminum frame gently curves upwards to support a fiberglass shade suspended over steel cable. In contrast, the lamp's painted stone base houses the transformer.

*Sapiens*

**1988**

An articulated task lamp, the sophisticated Sapiens was designed in-house by Sacha Ketoff, Paf, Milan, Italy. Made of black or grey aluminum, this double intensity halogen luminaire can be clamped to the table; it is distributed in the United States by Koch and Lowy Inc., Long Island City, New York.

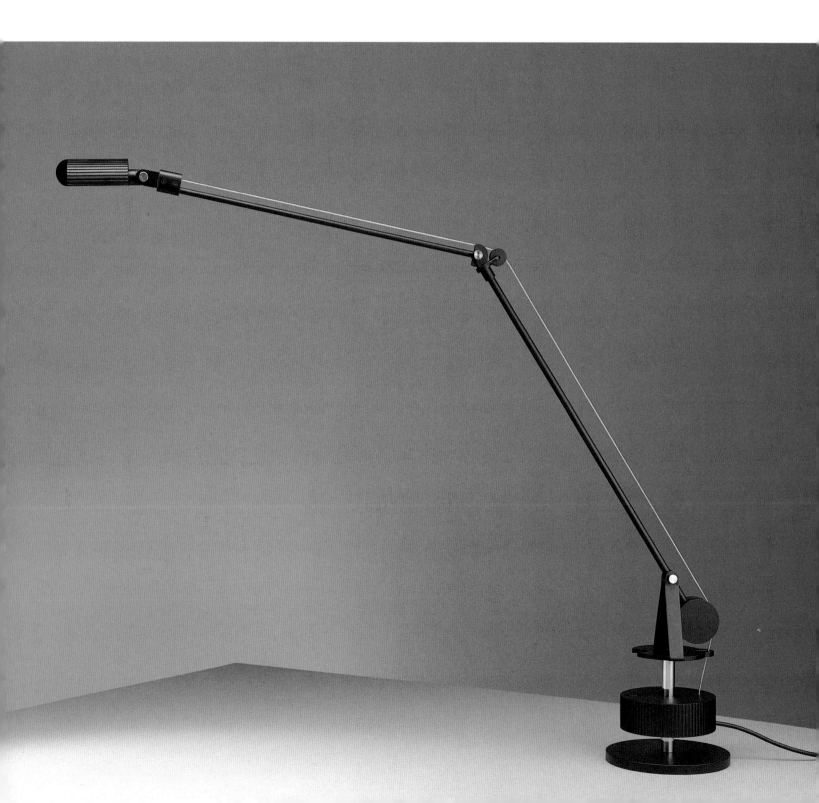

*Focus*

**1989**

Designed by Bruno Gecchelin for i Guzzini, Milan, Italy, Focus is a dichroic spotlight with a turned aluminum joint and a thermoplastic load bearing housing. The lamp attaches, by means of a curved support, to a low-voltage monophase track designed for exhibition spaces. A rod extends from the lamp fixture and can be fitted with colored glass to create a number of effects.

## *Sigla 1*

**1985**
**Base diameter 16cm x Height 75cm x Length 80cm**

A structural fiberglass conductor and a nylon joint allow this lamp to lock into different positions. Sigla 1 was designed by Rene Kemna, Delft, The Netherlands, for Sirrah S.p.A., Imola, Italy.

*Saeta*

**1988**

Designed in-house by Josep Llusca of Blauet S.A., Barcelona, Spain, Saeta, a halogen floor or table lamp, has an adjustable arm and shade, and is made of steel with a silver-bath finish; its base is made of black polyurethane.

## *Aero*

**1989**
**Height 15in x Length 32in x Width 4in**

This geometric assemblage of curved and parallel rod supports, cylindrical feet and counterbalanced shapes creates a desk lamp that provides a strong and direct down light. Designed and produced by James Evanson, New York, Aero is made of steel with baked powder-coated black epoxy finish.

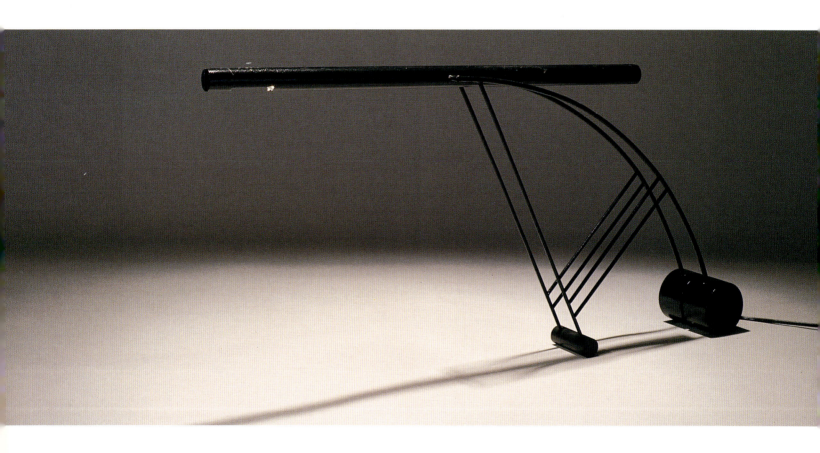

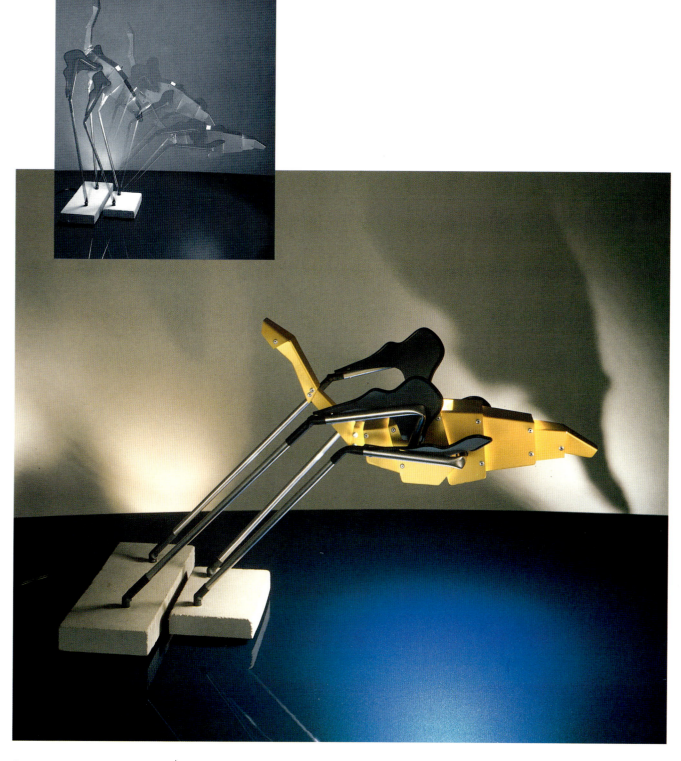

## Scaragoo

**1988**
**Maximum height 850mm**

Stefan Lindfors of Helsinki, Finland, has created a fanciful creature as a source of light. Looking like a great golden insect perched on long frail legs, this halogen table lamp made of plastic and metal explores the expression of color, shape and movement: the lamp moves and lights up as you touch it. Scaragoo is produced by Design M Ingo Maurer GmbH, Munich, West Germany.

## Hopper

Designed and produced by
Peter Krouwel of Ninaber/
Peters/Krouwel, Delft, The
Netherlands, Hopper is a
simple yet sophisticated
flourescent desk lamp made
of extruded aluminum.

**1985**
**Height 580mm**

## *Papiro*

**1988**
**Height 1900mm**

Like a tranquil forest, these tall and sinewy copper floor lamps cast cool, organic shadows upon their surroundings. The Papiro lamps were designed by Sergio Calatroni of Milan, Italy, for Bruna Socetti, also of Milan.

*Vienna 1900*

**1986**
**20in x 20in**

Inspired by early twentieth century Viennese design, this halogen desk lamp is made of satin aluminum with chrome details, a mesh top and a frosted glass insert. Vienna 1900 was designed by Robert Sonneman of Sonneman Design Group, Long Island City, New York, and manufactured by George Kovacs Lighting Inc., New York.

*On "Taro" "Giro"*

1 9 8 8
Width 290mm x Depth 150mm x Height 520mm

Designer Toshiyuki Kita of IDK Design Laboratory Ltd., Osaka, Japan and artist Keith Haring, New York mixed urban primitvism with high technology to create On "Taro" "Giro," an electroluminescent lamp mounted between glass and supported by a rock. The lamp is manufactured by Kreon, Antwerp, Belgium.

Focus on:

*Fantomas*

by David Baird

*"Our goal is to make beautiful objects—that way they are more useful."*

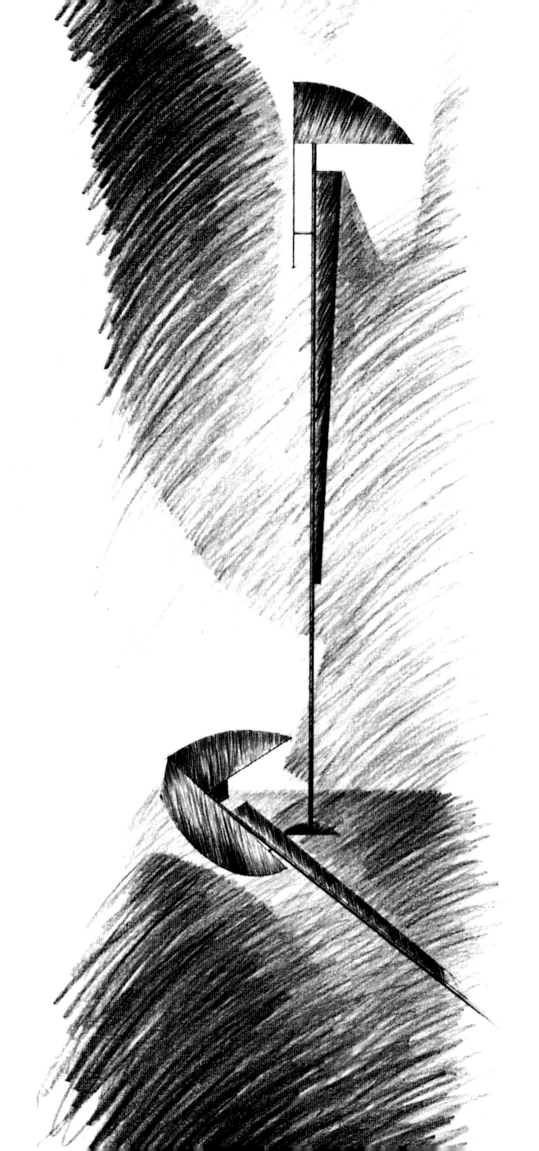

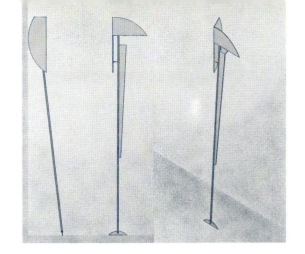

## Fantomas

**1988**
**Height 72in x Width 12in x Depth 12in**

A sculptural lamp that functions as both sconce and floor lamp, the six-foot-tall Fantomas leans "like a fugitve" against the wall. The lamp's asymmetric form makes a sleek, sharp silohuette against a background of light radiating in oblique directions. Designed and produced by David Baird of Ziggurat in La Jolla, California, the lamp is distributed in Europe by the French company Roche-Bobois. Fantomas is made of stamped sheet metal and is hand finished in black, zinc, ferrous or verdigris. Inexpensive yet elegant, the lamp was designed so that it could be locally produced by subcontractors and assembled by clients using rivet guns, arbor presses and screwdrivers.

# Interview

*David Baird graduated from the University of Tennessee in 1979 with a degree in architecture. In 1983 he formed Ziggurat, a design collaborative based in La Jolla, California, which now includes artists and designers from various professions. Their projects have ranged from architecture to graphic design; they have recently completed mass-produced lighting and furniture pieces that have received several design and craft awards. Fantomas received an award in the 1989 ID Annual Design Review.*

**How was the project initiated?** As with most of our designs, Fantomas was initiated as a speculative business venture. Not only did we design and develop the lamp but we also manufacture and distribute it. **How were you influenced or inspired?** Fantomas was influenced by my interest in abstract sculpture and the human body. It was also inspired by, and named after, a nefarious phantom character seen on French television in the fifties. **Did you use any special materials or technology?** We used economical materials such as cold rolled steel and stamped sheet metal. The rich finishes of oxidized copper and steel were applied by hand; this is a way of linking our work, which is mass produced, to sculpture. **Does this lamp have any special function or purpose?** All our lamps are designed for ambient lighting. Our goal is to make beautiful objects; that way they are more useful. **What was the biggest obstacle?** Working on perfecting the finishes. **Evaluate the success of your design.** Fantomas is now manufactured in Europe by Luminaires Lucien Gau. It is distributed exclusively through Europe by Roche-Bobois, a French company with over two hundred furniture showrooms in Europe. We are also producing the lamp for market in the United States and Canada. **What would you like to design next?** Right now we have four new lamps in production. Ironically, because of my success with lighting and furniture, I am now beginning to receive more architectural commissions. Ultimately, I would like to collaborate with a more sophisticated manufacturer to produce the backlog of other designs I have already developed. **What is the future of lighting design?** I have no idea. I am just trying to make beautiful objects for people to use and enjoy.

*Taraxacum*

**1988**

An explosion of finely blown glass bubbles, Taraxacum replaces classic chandeliers with a system of multiple light bulbs. Designed by Achille Castiglioni, Milan, Italy, this icosahedron, or twenty-sided object, consists of twenty hinged, bright aluminum triangles, each holding three Globolux clear bulbs. Taraxacum is produced by Flos Inc., Huntington Station, New York.

## Sardine Light

**1987**
15in x 5in x 2¼in

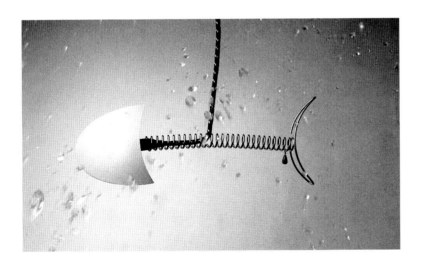

Combining zoomorphic form with utility materials—a coiled steel spine and a folded fiberglass head—the Sardine Light hangs from the ceiling by its electrical cord; its incandescent light is aimed by adjusting the lamp's fulcrum or lead weight. The lamp was designed by Tucker Viemeister and Lisa Krohn, Smart Design, New York, for Gallery 91, New York.

## U19

**1 9 8 4**
**Height 58in x Width 10in x Depth 14in**

U19 was designed and produced by Randall Toltzman of Fischerconcepts, Scottsdale, Arizona. With a striking formed aluminum silhouette and a uni-directional lamp housing that rotates 360 degrees, the U19 floor lamp can be used as a reading lamp or an uplight.

**_Via_**

---

**1989**

Via is an inventive track lighting system designed by Bruck of West Germany for Artup Lighting of Santa Ana, California. Fixture heads magnetically attach to the stainless steel track, which can either be suspended from the ceiling or flush-mounted. Low-voltage power is transmitted directly from the track through the stainless steel fixtures, eliminating the need for wiring.

Casting spectacular shadows on the walls and ceiling, the Four Button Luminario was inspired by the eerie lanterns of the Pueblo Indians from central New Mexico. Designed and fabricated by Mark Parrish, Parrish Designs, Brooklyn, New York, the lamp's shade comes in either woven copper, brass, bronze or stainless steel and the base is made from cast black iron.

**1989**
**Height 43in; Base 5in x 5in**

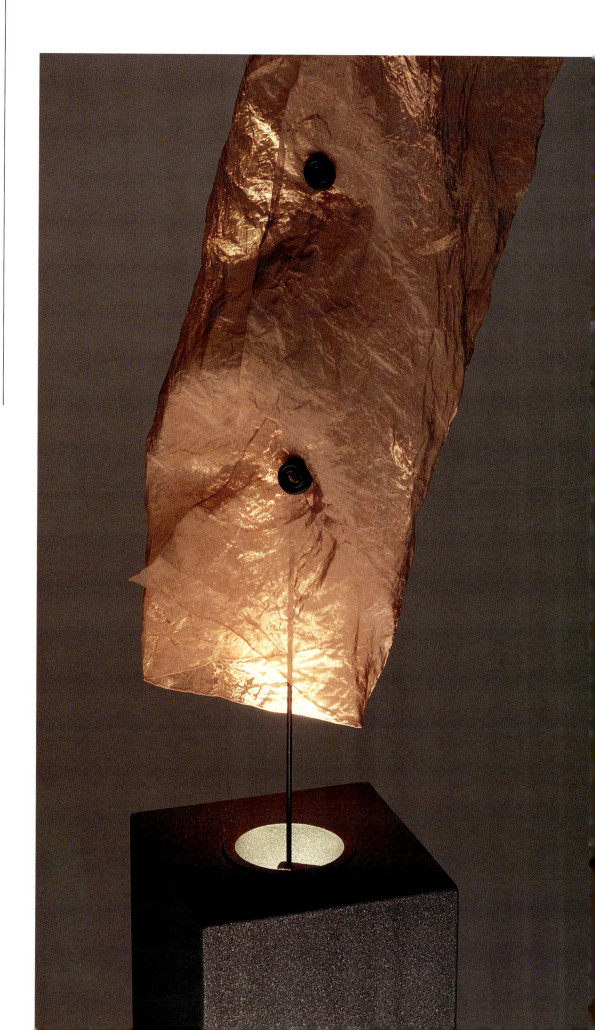

*Tiramisu*

**1988**
**2000mm x 400mm x 650mm**

An eclectic mixture of form and function, Tiramisu is an incandescent floor lamp designed by Roberto Marcatti, Milan, Italy and manufactured by Noto, also of Milan. The lamp is made of a steel tube finished in black epoxy, with two rubber tires, and incandescent light bulb and plasma-cut metal wings.

## Lazylight

**1988**

Operated electronically, this halogen table lamp houses a transformer and motor in its base. When the motor is switched on, cables flex the lamp's black thermoplastic arm, shortening or lengthening it for the desired lighting position. Lazylight was designed by Paolo Francesco Piva, Studio Dada, Milan, Italy, and manufactured by Luxo S.p.A., Presezzo, Italy.

# *Galileo*

**1988**
**Height 2000mm x Base 300mm X 300mm**

Designed and produced by Alroy 10, Tel-Aviv, Israel, Galileo is a halogen floor lamp made of stamped sheet steel, mild steel square tubing, and a cast-iron, wood or ceramic base, all finished in matt black epoxy paint.

# *Joia*

**1986**
**Height 260mm x Diameter 380mm**

A ceiling-mounted lamp, Joia bounces halogen rays off its white disc-shaped reflector to flood the room with indirect light. The lamp, designed in-house by Josep Llusca for Metalarte, Barcelona, Spain is comprised of a white lacquered disc from which a chromium-plated fixture is suspended.

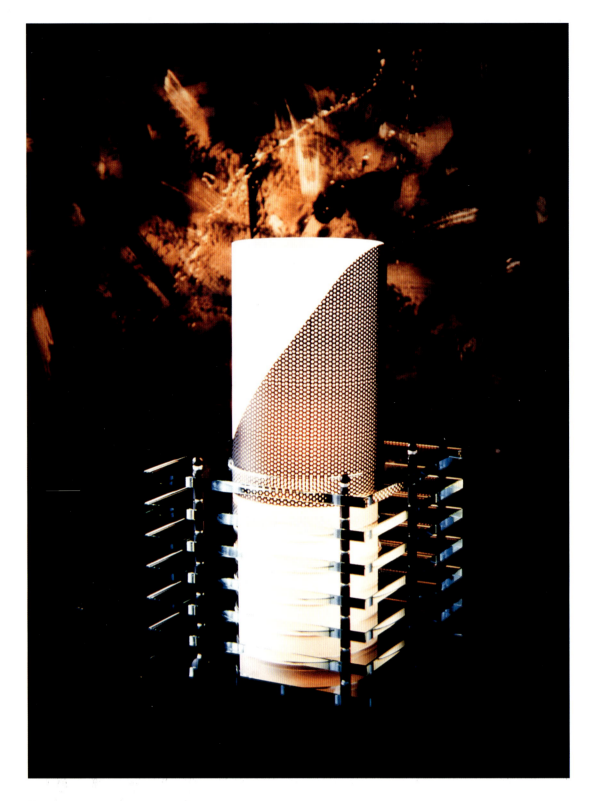

*Formosa*

**1988**
**425mm x 240mm x 240mm**

Supported by a stack of finely treated crystal or copper slabs, Formosa, a table lamp, houses an incandescent bulb diffused by a cylinder of frosted pyrex glass. Surrounding the glass is a black painted metal screen that swivels around the diffuser's circumference, changing the mood and orientation of the light. Formosa was designed by Roberto Marcatti and Alfonso Crotti of Roberto Marcatti Architetto & Associates, Milan, Italy, and is manufactured by Ar Far Studio Luce, also of Milan.

## *Palio*

**1985**
**Width 13.8in x Height 15.7in**

Palio diffuses soft incandescent light from its cylindrical opal glass body and contoured reflector. Made of aluminum, chrome-plated brass and formed glass, the table lamp was designed by Perry King and Santiago Miranda for Atelier International Lighting, Long Island City, New York.

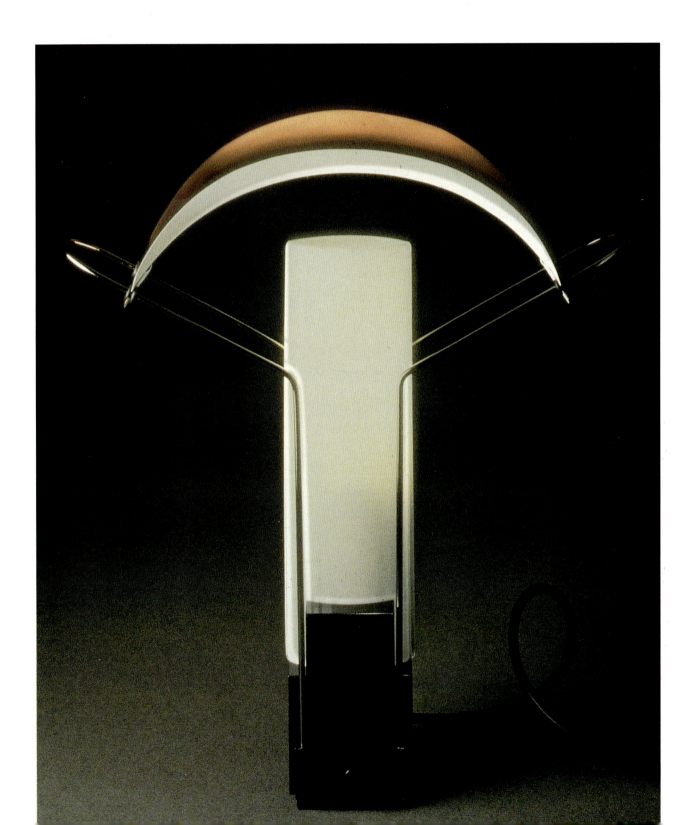

## Starry Skies

**1986**
**Diameter 12in x Height 15 in**

Made of aluminum kitchen colanders finished with gold auto paint and outfitted with hung silver tip lamps, Starry Skies reflect sparkle patterns onto the ceiling and walls. These cleverly fabricated incandescent ceiling lamps were designed in-house by Frederic Schwartz, Anderson/Schwartz, New York.

## Yanagi

**1988**
**24in x 6in**

Designed and fabricated by Masciocchi and Merich, New York, for the Archetype Gallery, New York, Yanagi, a halogen table lamp, was inspired by traditional Japanese lighting and was realized in fiberglass, porcelain and steel.

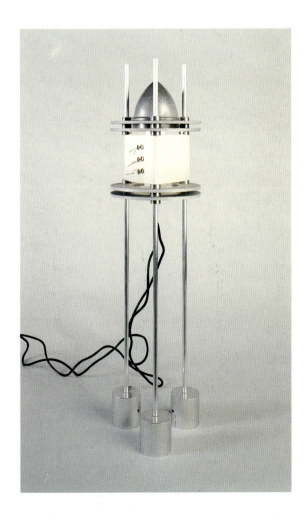

# Monolith

by Brian Stewart

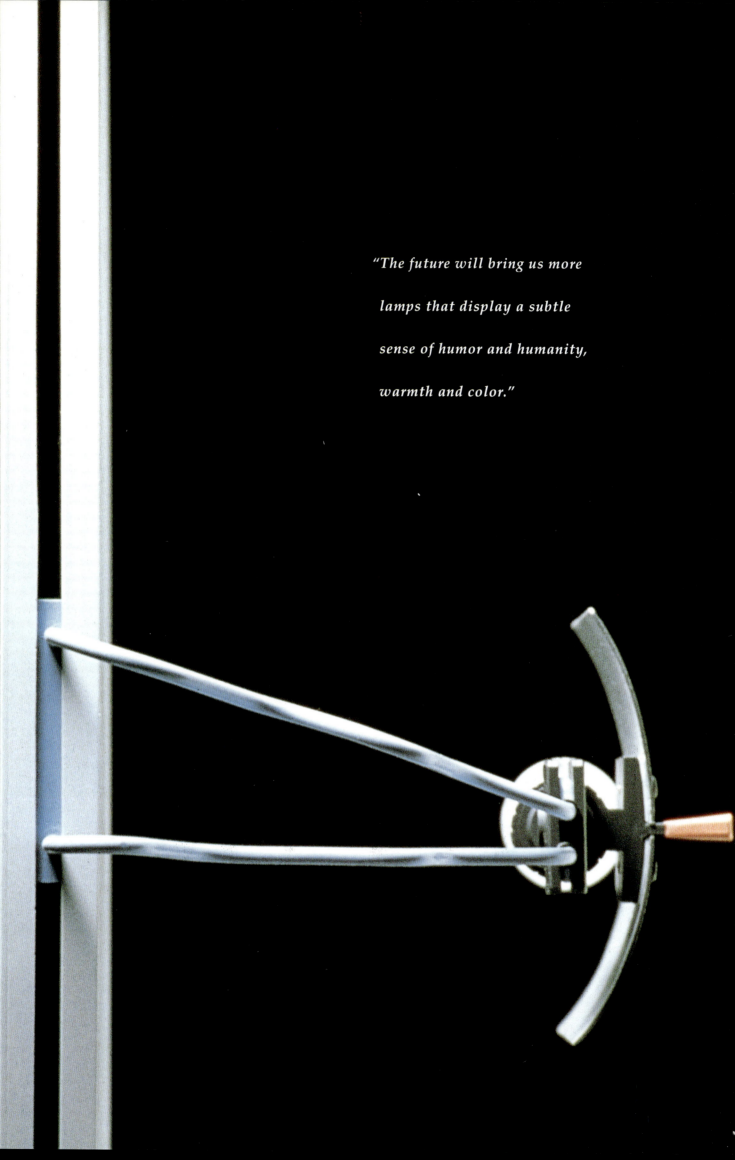

*"The future will bring us more lamps that display a subtle sense of humor and humanity, warmth and color."*

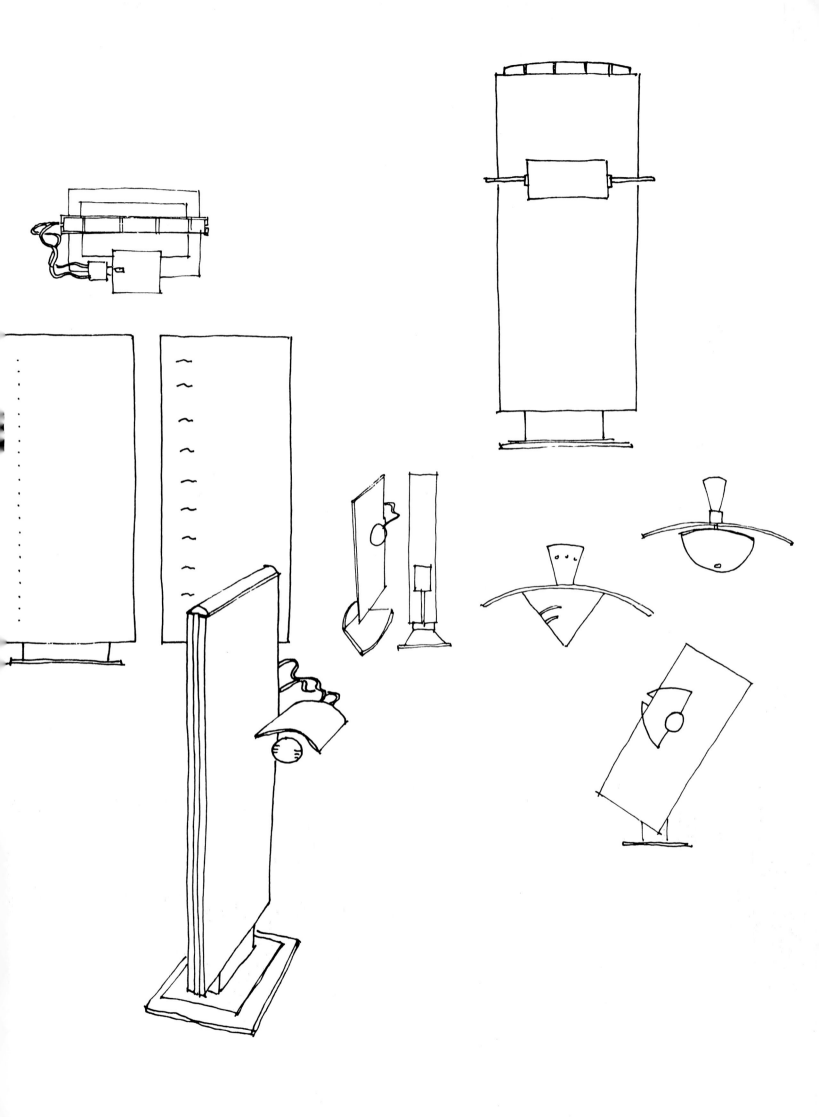

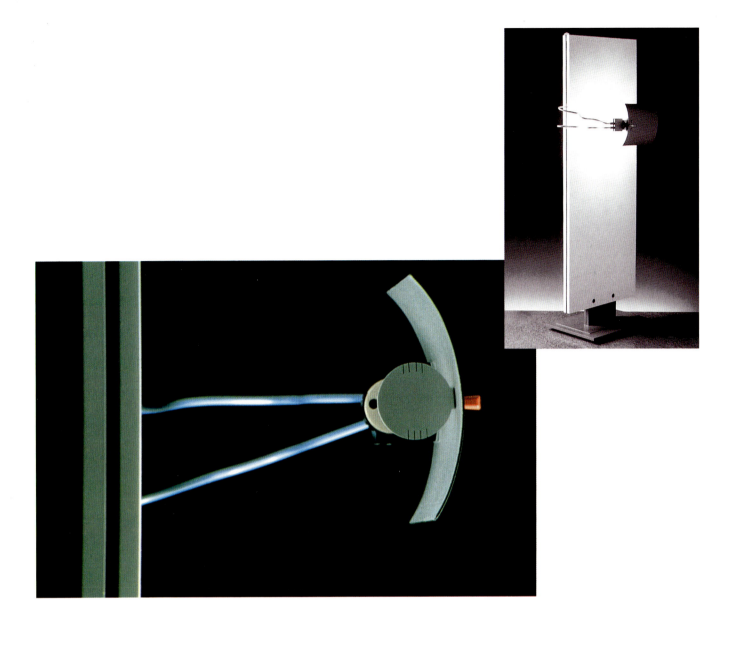

## Monolith Light

**1987**
**Height 21.5in x Width 7.5in x Depth 7in**

This dramatic low-voltage table lamp was designed with meticulous attention given to every detail, from its graceful form to the subtle characteristics of the light it reflects. The lamp's broad aluminum back plane creates a reflective surface that disperses the light and produces a soft glow of indirect light. The light fixture, housed in a casing that echoes the form of the back plane, slides vertically up and down, shining light on the full length of the back drop. Electrical leads are encased in support rods cleverly formed to look like the wavy lines of electricity—they are also the means by which the lamp is adjusted. Made of cast and extruded aluminum, molded plastic and pressed and formed steel, the Monolith light was designed in-house by Brian Stewart of ID Two, San Francisco, California.

# Interview

*Now vice-president of ID Two in San Francisco, Brian Stewart received his Bachelors degree in visual studies from Dartmouth College, Hanover, New Hampshire. As a senior designer at ID Two, Stewart has designed lighting, consumer and medical products, and corporate product design guidelines. His work has appeared in numerous publications including ID, Domus, Designweek, New American Design and Product Design 3.*

**How was the project initiated?** The Monolith light was designed in response to a competition sponsored by an English lighting manufacturer. **How were you influenced or inspired?** I wanted to design a light fixture that would reflect the delicate minimalism of halogen bulb technology. Wires leading to these low voltage bulbs do not need to be insulated. I wanted to take advantage of this by inviting the user to touch the wires. Therefore, the support rods that conduct current to the lamp also allow the user to adjust the position of the lamp. Another influence was light. It is invisible. It becomes interesting when it reflects off a surface, when it cast shadows on itself. **Did you use any special materials or technology?** I used materials and processes appropriate for the function of each part of the lamp. The small and relatively complex bulb housing is a plastic injection molding, as is the cap on the back plane. The shade is fabricated from sheet metal, the back pane is an aluminum extrusion with an integral track to provide vertical adjustment, and the base was cast for weight and stability. **What alternatives were explored?** I considered using ceramics, glass or aluminum sheeting for the broad planar structure. I rejected these in favor of an extrusion, which allowed me to form a vertical track right into the structure. I considered using the track to conduct current along its length but decided on a simpler approach where the electrical leads float inside the hollow back plane with enough wire to allow the light support to move over the whole length of the track.

**What would you like to design next?** I would like to design a low cost lamp using standard incandescent bulbs and fixtures. There seem to be few affordable, interesting lamps available that use the regular old lightbulb. **What is the future of lighting design?** "Designer" lighting shops today are overflowing with serious, black, oppressively elegant and often expensive products. Many of these are wonderful designs, but I hope the future will bring us more lamps that display a subtle sense of humor and humanity, warmth and color.

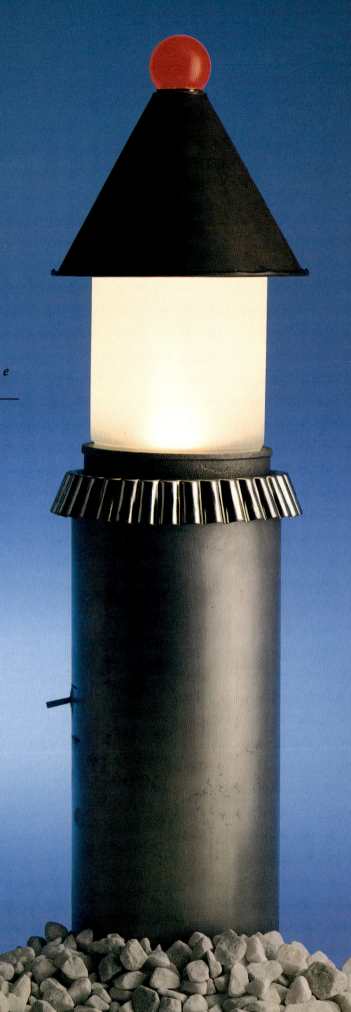

### *Lighthouse*

**1988**
**6in x Height 20in**

Inspired by Edward Hopper's lighthouse paintings, this incandsescent table lamp was designed and produced by Frederic Schwartz of Anderson/Schwartz, New York. Radiating soft diffused light, Lighthouse is made from readily available, specially treated materials like sandblasted aluminum pipe, sandblasted glass bell jars and patinated tin shades.

## *Mackinaw 900*

**1986**
**Diameter 22in**

Simply fabricated of spun aluminum with a half-sphere accent of glass, and suspended from the ceiling by aircraft cable, this incandescent up-light was designed by Larry Lazin of Lazin Lighting, New York.

## Arcade

Part of the Zeus Collection manufactured by Noto SRL, Milan, Italy, Arcade is a halogen table or floor lamp made of iron rod finished in black epoxy paint. This anthropomorphically shaped lamp houses adjustable floodlights in its beak-shaped reflectors and was designed by Roberto Marcatti of Lavori in Corso, also in Milan.

**1986**
Table lamp: 650mm x 150mm x 630mm;
Floor lamp: 660mm x 200mm x 1300mm

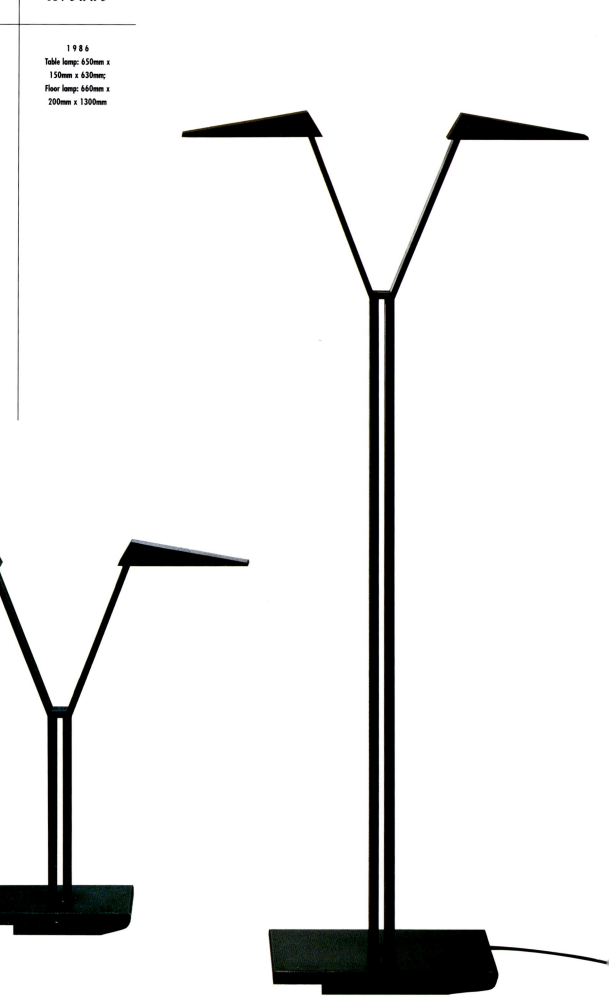

## Tilt 36

**1987**
**Height 24in, 30in, 36in, or 42in x Diameter 11³/₈in**

Designed in-house by Doyle Crosby, Boyd Lighting, San Francisco, California, this ceiling fixture hovers like a spaceship, its angle controlled by four balanced and adjustable suspension cables. The lamp's incandescent bulb is sandwiched between two aluminum discs finished in satin, brass, or silver granite.

*Nessie*

1989

Inspired by the mythical Loch Ness monster which this lamp's lacquered anodized body resembles, Nessie is a suspension lamp that provides direct and indirect lighting. Five dichroic bulbs are housed on the crests and troughs of the lamp body, which is available in black or grey. Nessie was designed by De Pas, D'Urbino and Lomazzi, Milan, Italy, and produced by Stilnovo, also of Milan

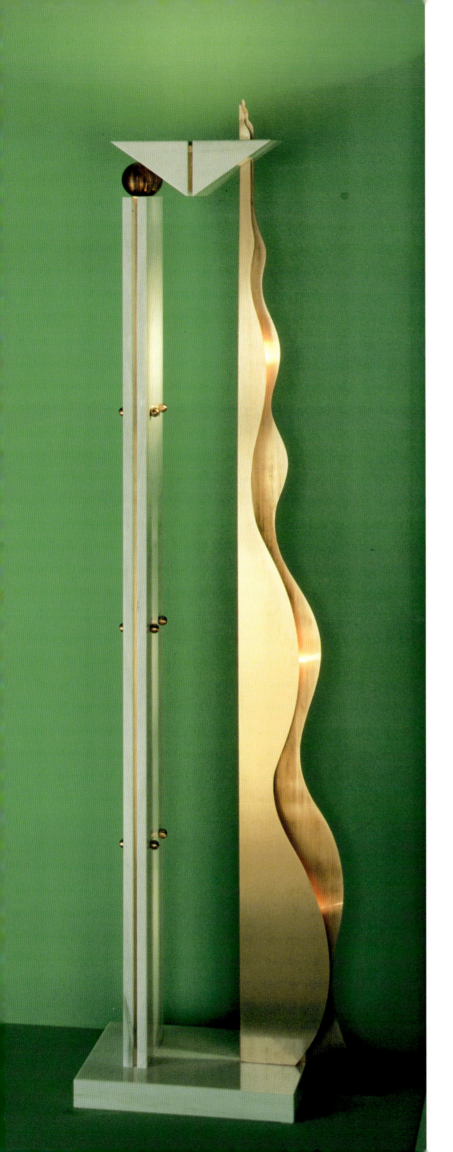

## *Dea*

**1 9 8 8**
**Base: 450mm x 350mm x 55mm;**
**Height 2000mm**

With a marble base anchoring two distinctive posts—one a hard-edged marble rectangle, the other sensuously curved copper sheets—Dea is a sculptural floor lamp with three vertically oriented halogen bulbs that can be regulated for different effects. The lamp was designed by Tiziano Cuberli of Marmoluce, Oberengstringen, Switzerland.

## Lamp #1

**1987**
**Height 16in x Length 25 5/8in x Width 6 5/16in**

This finely finished construction, made up of polished aluminum bars, pegs and rods, was designed by Lawrence Laske of Laske Design Group, New York. Lamp #1 can be vertically adjusted by moving a peg up or down a series of holes drilled into the support elements; the back of the arm is fixed to the base pivoting at its center.

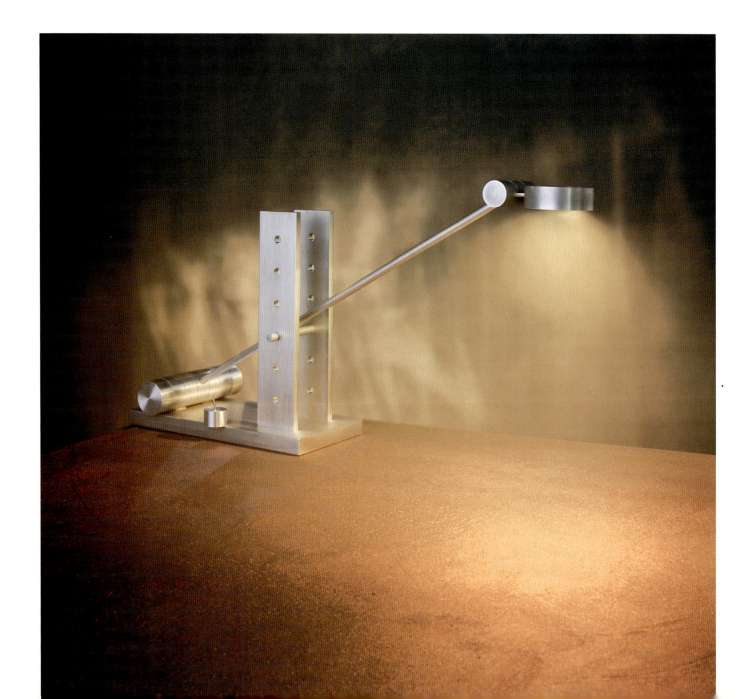

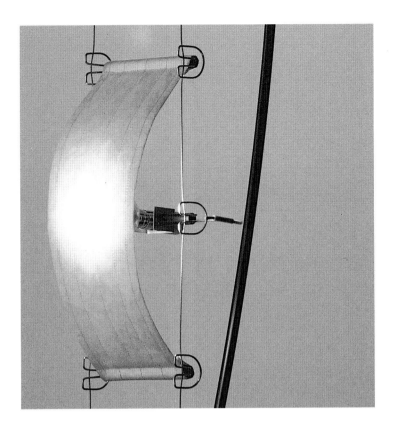

## Sail

**1986**
**Height 1820mm x Base diameter 210mm**

Evoking images of a ship's mast supporting a tiny billowing sail, this lamp is a flexible illumination system that allows interchange between the light source and diffuser, which slide up and down their supporting rod. Designed by Miles Keller and produced by Kerr Keller Design, Toronto, Canada, Sail has a concrete base, tyvek and fiberglass shades and FRD rod support column.

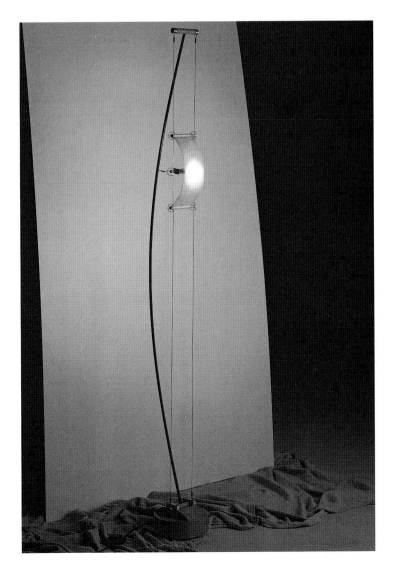

## *Sette Magie*

**1988**
**Height 240 or 200cm x Diameter 28cm x Base diameter 51cm**

A metallic cylindrical floor lamp finished in micaceous iron grey or gold or silver leaf, Sette Magie contains two reflectors that slide inside the cylinder and cast light of differing intensities and color depending on their position. This halogen lamp was designed by Lella and Massimo Vignelli, New York, for Morphos, Bergamo, Italy.

## Mercur

**1988**
1000mm x 200mm x 200mm

An impressive geometric assemblage, Mercur suspends from the ceiling; its light source, hidden behind the silhouette of a black triangle, reflects abundant light off an arc of aluminum sheeting. The fixture was designed by Vladimir Pezdirc, Ljubljana, Yugoslavia, and manufactured by Kvadrat, also of Ljubljana.

This towering architectural floor lamp is made of painted, perforated steel and incorporates three fluorescent tubes stacked end to end. Chicago Tribune was designed by Matteo Thun, Milan, Italy, and manufactured by Bieffeplast, Caselle Di Selvazzano, Italy.

**1985**
**300mm x 300mm x 1900mm**

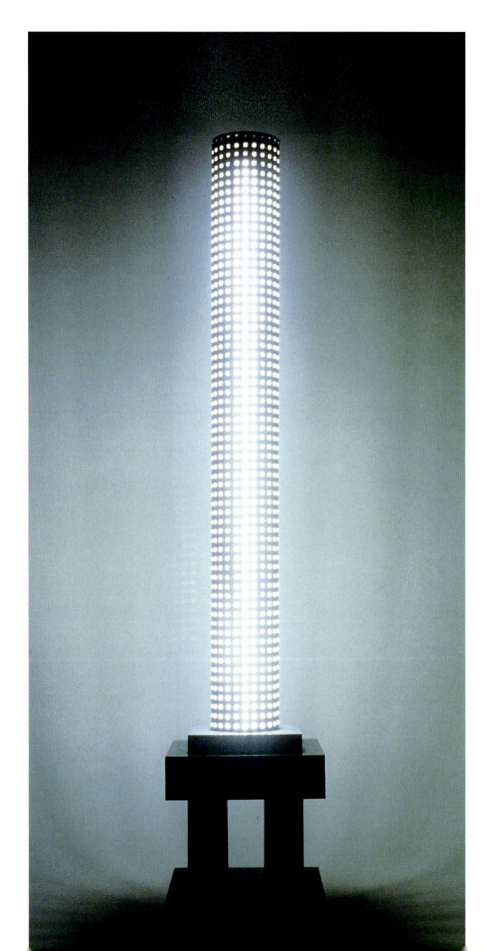

## Lighted by
## the Blinds

**1989**
**72in x 14in x 14in**

Standing tall on a wooden pedestal, Lighted by the Blinds is a limited production floor lamp made of aluminum levelors that can be manipulated for a variety of effects. The lamp was designed and fabricated by Terence Leong, New York.

**1988**

A flexible range of lighting for the wall, table or floor, the Manhattan Series is efficiently constructed so that all versions are manufactured using the same tooling. The lamp's most striking element is its central glass disc diffuser: a hole in its center lets light through while a textured ring etched on its surface absorbs the surrounding rays. The lamphead rotates over 135 degrees and lamp supports are made of dark-grey polycarbonate; all metal parts are laquered in a dark-grey metallic finish. The Manhattan Series was designed in-house by Robert Blaich and Alfred Van Elk, Philips Lighting, Eindhoven, The Netherlands.

*Tower 001*

1988
250mm x 500mm

Inspired by the urban architectural landscape, Maurizio Favetta of Thun Associates, Milan, Italy, has created a tower-like table lamp out of ceramics. Incandescent light radiates from "windows" on the surface and the top of the lamp. Tower 001 is produced by Viba, Cassola, Italy.

## *Modi:Terra*

**1986**
**Height 1800mm**

This refined and simple halogen floor lamp sparks with personality. With an articulated rubber neck and spun aluminum reflector, Modi:Terra was designed by Toshiyuki Kita of IDK Design Laboratory Ltd., Osaka, Japan, and manufactured by Luci S.p.A., Milan, Italy.

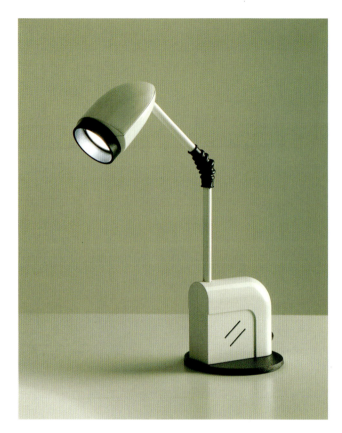

# Light Tapestry

**1985**
**13.5in x 8in**

Using an optical projection lens plate and a one-piece cast-glass defraction system, this tiny wall sconce projects a dramatic fan of light rays onto the wall; its halogen lamp is simply housed in a polished brass or chrome body. The sconce was designed by Jerome H. Simon of Architectural Arts & Technology, Boston, Massachusetts, for Nessen Lamps Inc., Port Chester, New York.

Focus on:

*Space II*

by Pascal Luthi

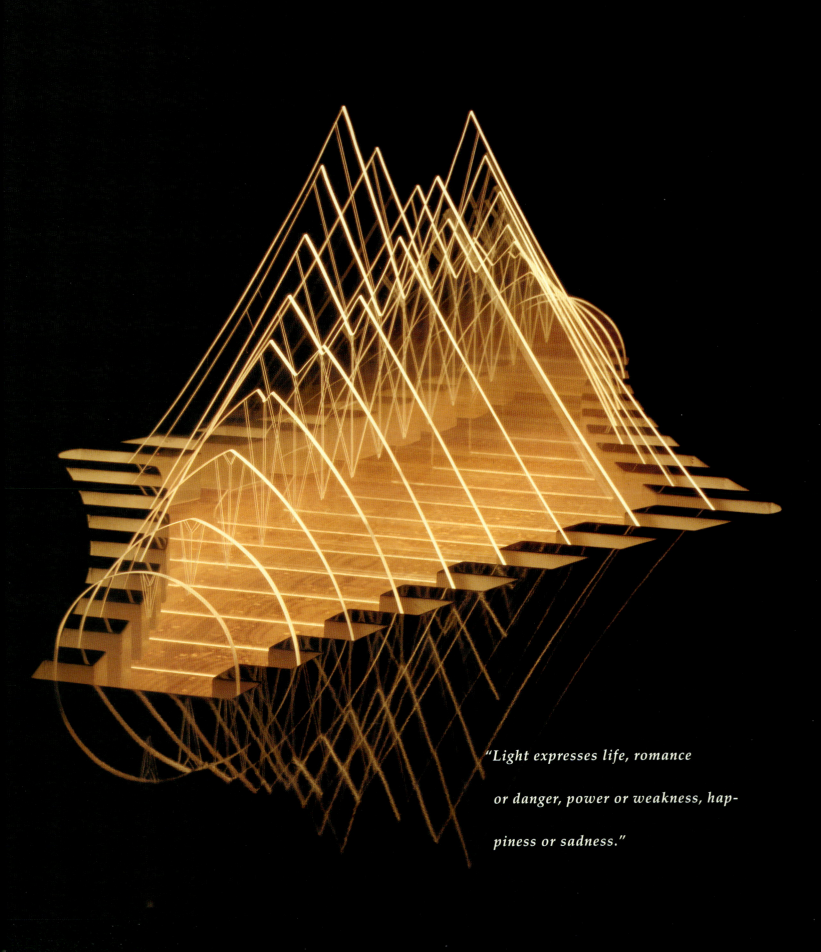

"Light expresses life, romance or danger, power or weakness, happiness or sadness."

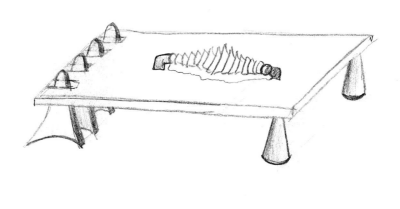

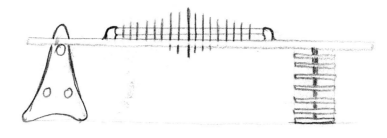

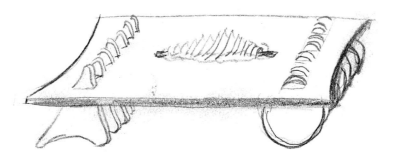

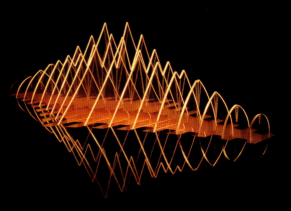

**1988**
**Height 40in x Length 20in x Width 25in**

This eerie but beautiful skeletal form that looms toward the viewer from its dark background is simply an incandescent wall lamp made of illuminated sheets of plexiglass and black lacquered wood. The lamp's plexiglass sheets are mounted in evenly spaced rows over a thin veneer of bird's-eye-maple and are lit from behind by a 140 watt bulb. Light gently illuminates the plexiglass edges while shining up through the maple to highlight its delicate textures and patterns. Cleverly juxtaposing crafted finished woods with the angular and sharply transparent plexiglass, the designer, Pascal Luthi, has created a unique wall light. Space II is produced in-house by Maison Dupin, Geneva, Switzerland.

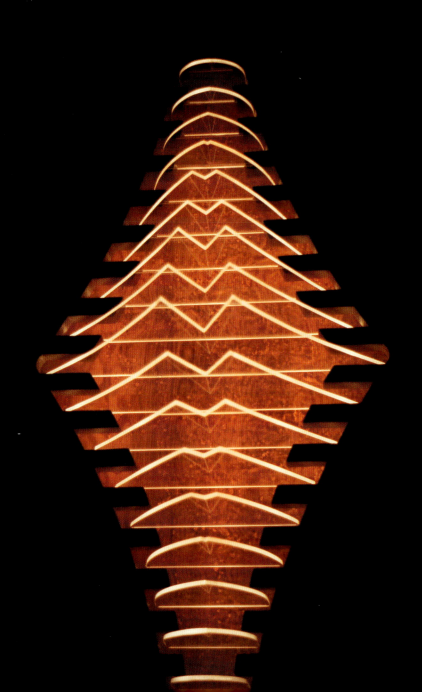

# Interview

*A graduate of the New York School of Interior Design and the Swain School of Design in Massachusetts, Pascal Luthi is a designer whose projects range from lighting and furniture to interiors. Luthi is partner at Maison Dupin, an interior design firm in Geneva, Switzerland, whose clients include the Chemical Bank, Van Cleef and Arpels and Boucheron. His work has received a number of awards, including the 1989 ID Annual Design Review award for his Union Chair.*

**How was the project initiated?** All my life I have been attracted to light. Light expresses life, romance, or danger, power or weakness, happiness or sadness. **How were you influenced or inspired?** I wanted to create a sculptural piece that would distribute atmospheric light. My idea was to contrast ancestral shapes with high-tech architectural elements. **Did you use any special materials or technology?** Space II uses a technique that I developed over the past two years. This process, patented internationally, allows light to pass through the surface of any kind of wood. The light illuminates hidden wood grain and the beautiful depth of its design. **What was the biggest obstacle?** The biggest obstacle was resolving all the technical problems of luminous wood. **Evaluate the success of your design.** The combination of the natural and luminous birds-eye-maple with the architectural plexiglass and the highly polished black lacquered wood is succesful in creating a high-tech yet romantic light. **What would you like to design next?** I would like to change the scale of my work. I have started to design a room with two walls facing each other. The room is treated like a sculpture using the same materials I used for Space II. Instead of looking at a luminous object, you will actually be inside it, a part of it. With new electronics, like body sensor switches, fiber optics and solid state electro-luminescent lamps, a psychological interaction will be established between people and the space. **What is the future of lighting design?** My goal is to design objects, furniture and interior space where light becomes a physical experience. Being able to change light and ambience of a space according to mood will give a new dimension to interior design.

Designed by Roberto Mar-
catti of Lavori in Corso,
Milan, Italy, the Circus halogen floor lamp creates a car-
nival ambience marked,
nontheless, by subtlety. The
lamp consists of an arched
steel frame that delicately
supports a floating glass diffuser positioned over an
upside down ceramic spherical cap. Circus is part of the
Zeus Collection manufac-
tured by Noto SRL, Milan.

**1988**
**Diameter 300mm x**
**Height 1950mm**

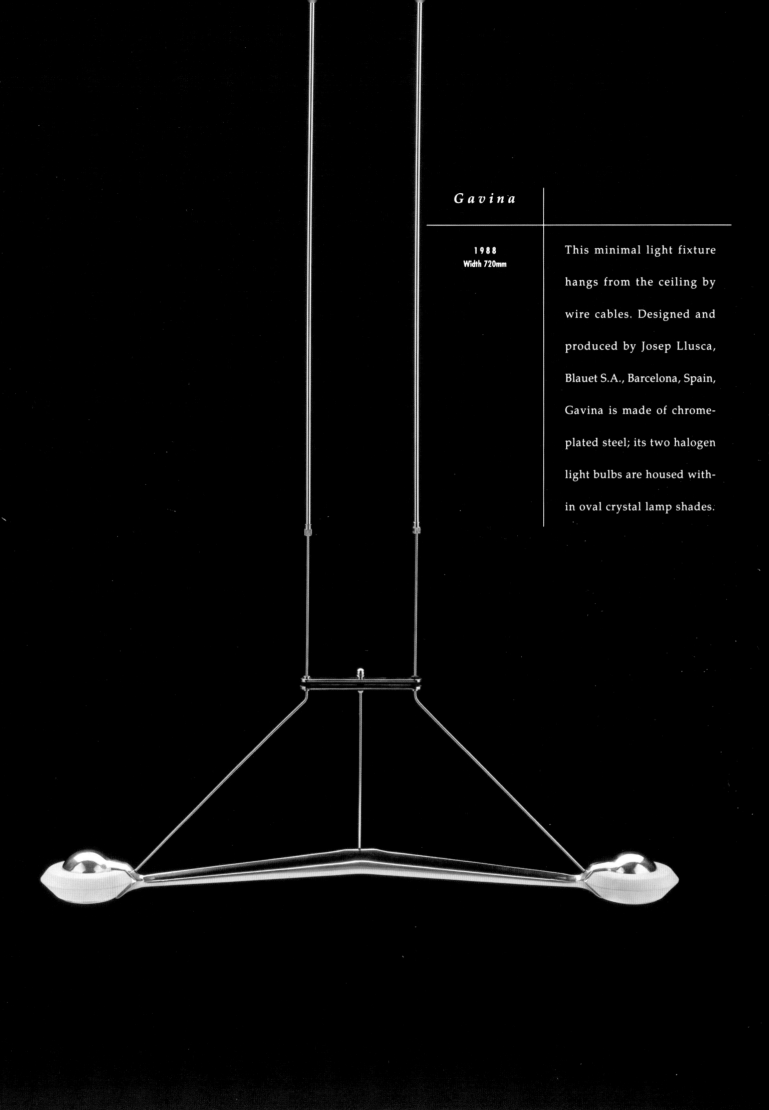

*Gavina*

**1988**
**Width 720mm**

This minimal light fixture hangs from the ceiling by wire cables. Designed and produced by Josep Llusca, Blauet S.A., Barcelona, Spain, Gavina is made of chrome-plated steel; its two halogen light bulbs are housed within oval crystal lamp shades.

## Dove

A classic, the low-voltage Dove halogen floor and desk lamps were designed by Mario Barbaglia and Marco Columbo of Paf, Milan, Italy. Made of technopolymer plastic in black, white, yellow, blue or red, this bird-like lamp rotates on its polished black metal base; its flexible arm and shade are easily adjustable. Dove is distributed in the United States by Koch + Lowy Inc., Long Island City, New York.

**1985**
Floor lamp: 53in x 33in; Desk lamp: 36in x 33in

_Ettore_

**1987**
12 5/sin x 66 7/sin

Radiating light from both ends, simultaneously or separately, the Ettore halogen floor lamp is made of black epoxy painted metal; its lower diffuser is made of red painted metal with an anti-dazzling grill. The lamp was designed by Ernesto Gismondi for Artemide Inc., Long Island City, New York.

*Urania*

**1985**
**2000mm x 450mm**

With the grace of the full moon, Urania, a floor lamp, stands tall and powerful, casting soft light through its white disc-shaped diffuser. The lamp's base is made of black epoxy-coated metal and its reflective disc rotates 360 degrees to spread light in all directions. Urania was designed and produced by Jorge Garcia Garay, Garcia Garay S.A., Barcelona, Spain.

# La Lune Sans Le Chapeau

**1987**
**Height 680mm**

This lightweight and inexpensive incandescent paper lamp stands with a flourish on three wire legs. La Lune Sans Le Chapeau was designed by Philippe Starck, Montfort L'Amaury, France, for Mail Order Catalog: 3 Suisses France, Croix, France.

1 9 8 8
83in x 30in x 27in

Like two haunted figures, the Voyager lamps, designed by Alex Locadia, New York,

for Art et Industrie, also of New York, appear as if they could actually walk. Made

from carved wood supported by a steel base, the twin lamps house halogen bulbs that

emit an eerie light from cast resin insets in the center of their bodies.

## Wall Sconces

**1988**
**Height 10 1/2in x Width 17in x Depth 17 1/2in**

Eric Margry and Mark Anderson of Art Lite, Alexandria, Virginia, designed and produced this series of lively lamps whose glass shades are painted in zebra and leopard skin prints and other bold, colorful patterns. The lamps' transformers are housed in painted wood fixtures.

**1988**
Base: 2³/₄in x 4in x 6³/₄in; Shade: 2in x 3¹/₄in x 6in; Arm length: 15³/₄in

With a bridge truss arm assembly and cable tensioning system that allows for full articulation, this mechanical looking lamp is simply made of a combination of plastics including glass filled nylon, ABS and polycarbonate. Stasis was designed and produced by Ralph Osterhout of Tekna Inc., Menlo Park, California.

## Burlington Desk Light

**1987**
**Height 515mm x Diameter 180mm**

The Burlington Desk Light is made up of a halogen lamp and an adjustable mirror elegantly housed within a blown glass enclosure that reduces glare and protects the user from heat generated by the electrical components. The lamp was designed by David Morgan Assoc., London, England for Panasonic, Osaka, Japan.

*Erco Oseris*

**1985**
**Diameter 4in x Length 8in**

The Erco Oseris is an angled, semi-spherical spot light that rotates 360 degrees on a vertical axis to precisely focus for different lighting situations. Made of formed metal, die-cast aluminum and injection molded plastic, these low voltage lamps were designed by Emilio Ambasz and Giancarlo Piretti, New York, for Erco Leuchten GmbH, Ludenschweid, West Germany.

*Tom*

1986
279 mm x 165mm

Concise and smartly detailed, Tom is a dichroic lighting fixture for the wall, ceiling or track. It has a polycarbonate body and shiny Ultem reflector; its small metal re-flector, which covers the halogen bulb, does not have to be removed for relamping. Tom was designed by Ezio Bellini for Targetti Sankey S.p.A., Florence, Italy.

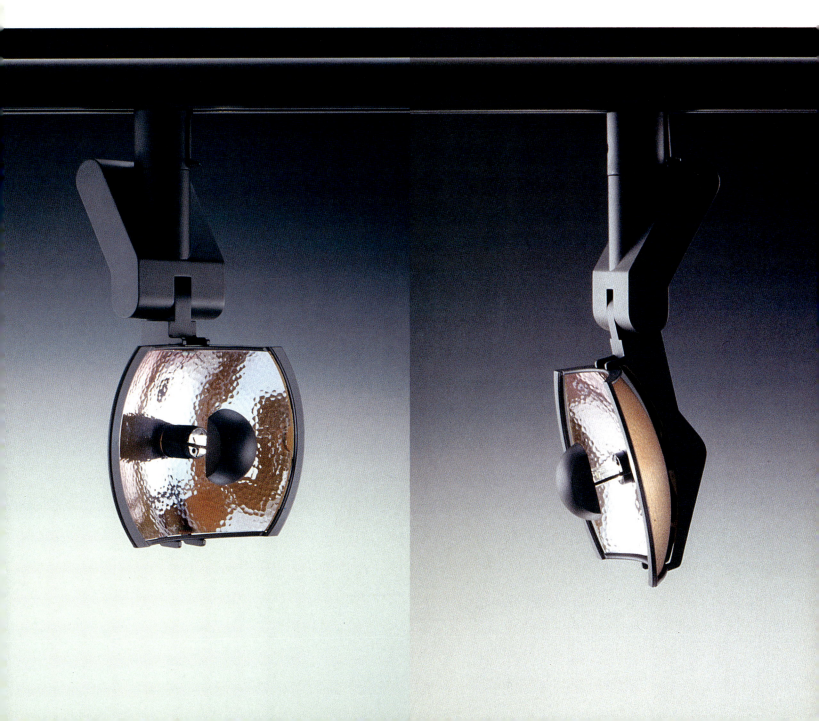

## *Strala*

**1986**
**Height 69 1/2in;**
**Base 4 1/2in x 4 1/2in**

Looking like a wizard with a pointed hat and a tall, spindly frame, Strala is a floor lamp designed and fabricated by Scot Laughton and Tom Deacon of Portico, Toronto, Canada. The lamp is turned on and dimmed by rotating a painted brass sphere; its spun aluminum cone, steel tube and base are all finished in matt black powder coated epoxy. "Strala" is Anglo-Saxon for a spear, javelin or beam of light.

## Crystal Needle

**1986**
**Height 77in x Width 22in x Depth 22in**

Crystal Needle looks like a towering monument of crystal, but is in fact a light fixture made of carved glass. The tungsten floor lamp stands on a cast concrete base, its surface etched with patterns. The lamp was designed by Terence Main, New York and is distributed by Art et Industrie, New York.

These delicate pendants of light made out of shiny steel hang from a metal bar suspended from the ceiling by cables. M6 was designed and produced by Jan Van Lierde, Kreon N.V., Antwerp, Belgium, and is distributed in the United States by the Modern Age Gallery, New York.

With parallel stainless steel rods supporting four adjustable halogen light fixtures, this low-voltage floor lamp was designed and produced by Mike Nutall, Matrix Product Design, Palo Alto, California.

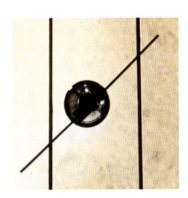

# Cascading Sconce

by Thomas Hucker

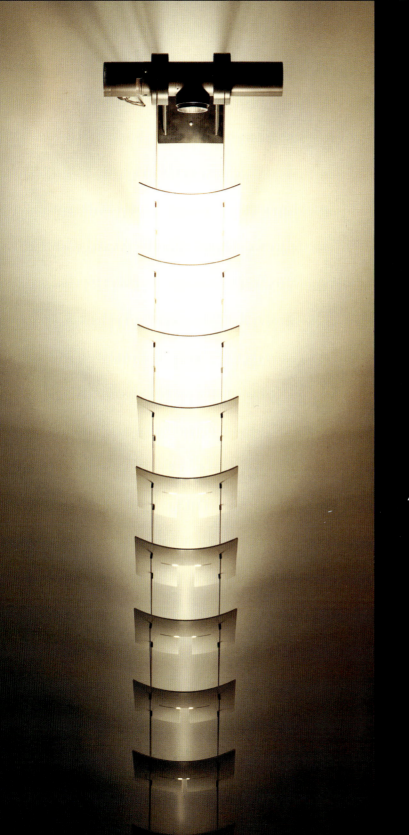

*"Creating a light source is*

*one specific and difficult*

*challenge; how the environment*

*reacts to it is another."*

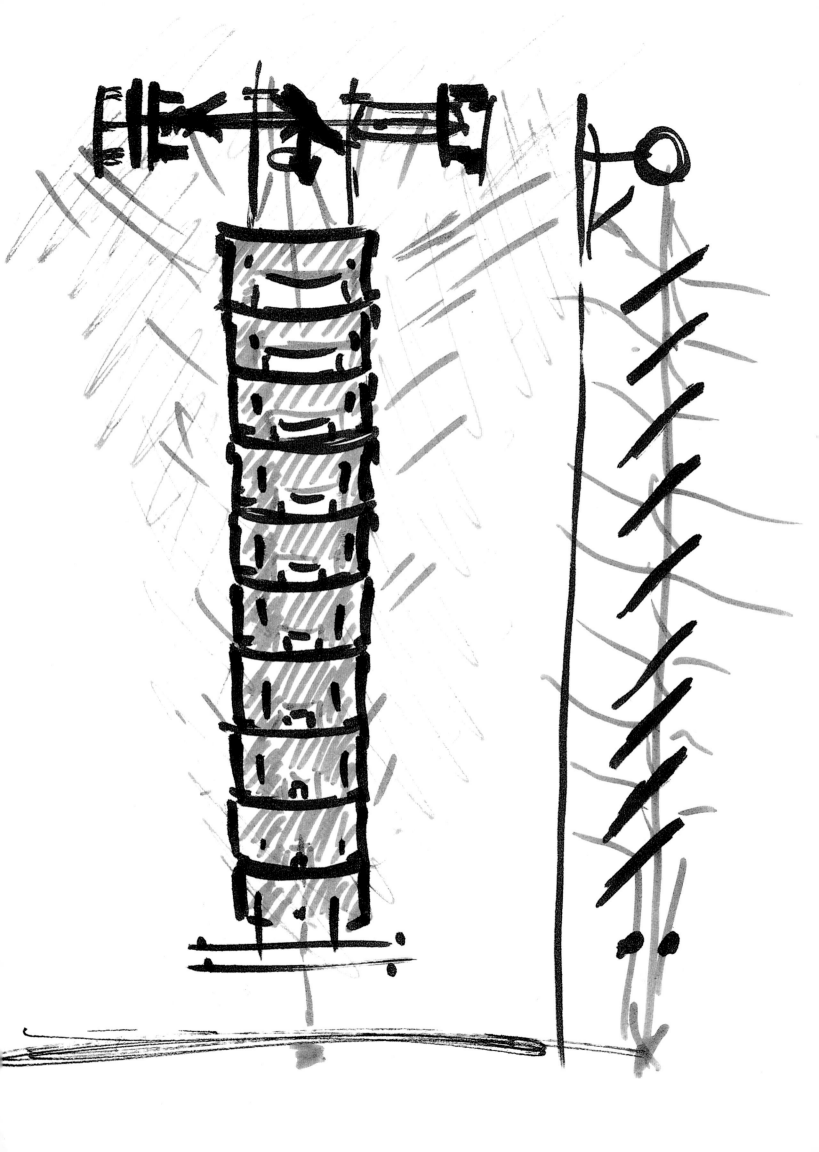

## Cascading Sconce

**1987**
**Height 72in x Length 20in x Depth 8in**

The Cascading Sconce, true to its name, is like a radiant waterfall of light. With physical and poetic grace, the Cascading Sconce gently manipulates and integrates light by passing it through a series of media. Designed and fabricated by Thomas Hucker, Charlestown, Massachusetts, the sconce is made up of a series of aluminum baffles hung horizontally and suspended vertically by cables attached to the top of the wall running all the way to the floor. As light rays pour down from the halogen source at the top, they are refracted through lenses and apertures cut into the baffles until finally, the beam is focused to a fifteen degree pinspot on the floor.

# Interview

*Thomas Hucker graduated from Boston University in 1980 with a certificate of mastery in furniture design and fabrication. In 1982 he was artist-in-residence at Tokyo Universtiy of Fine Arts, and in 1988 he was awarded a Fulbright-Hays scholarship and went on to study furniture design at Domus Academy, Milan, Italy, in 1989. A recipient of numerous awards, Hucker's Cascading Sconce was co-best of category in the 1987 ID Annual Design Review.*

**How was the project initiated?** The Cascading Sconce was initiated as an in-house exploration into the lighting arena. **How were you influenced or inspired?** The aesthetics of structural systems have always been of great interest to me. This became the theme for the sconce, which is a structure that would integrate and manipulate light as a medium. The louvers were the first elements on the drawing board because of their ability to block, reflect and segment light. After these were established, developing a collimated light source was the issue. The neutral grey for the louvers was chosen purely to reflect tones of light. As for a reference image, there is in some traditional Japanese buildings, a system for draining water where the water runs down chains instead of pipes - it reveals the passage of water in a most poetic way. **Did you use any special materials or technology?** There is really no new technology used. We run a low voltage 120-watt source through grey lacquered aluminum plates. The cuts in each plate create an aperture focus upon the plate below. **What was the biggest obstacle?** The biggest obstacle was venting the heat generated by the light source without leaking the light and airflow from behind the baffles. **What alternatives were explored?** Because the project was speculative, many decisions were made spontaneously. As there were only three weeks between concept and working prototype, we really did not know what to expect until the first prototype was turned on. **What would you like to design next?** I would like to explore new ways of manipulating light by exploring the relationship between light and new light-responsive materials. I would like to create a system where the structure, not the light source, is of visual importance. **What is the future of lighting design?** Lighting design obviously owes much to the technological inventiveness of companies like Osram, Sylvania and Philips. However, there is also a growing interest in how materials interact with light. Creating a light source is one specific and difficult challenge. How the environment reacts to it is another.

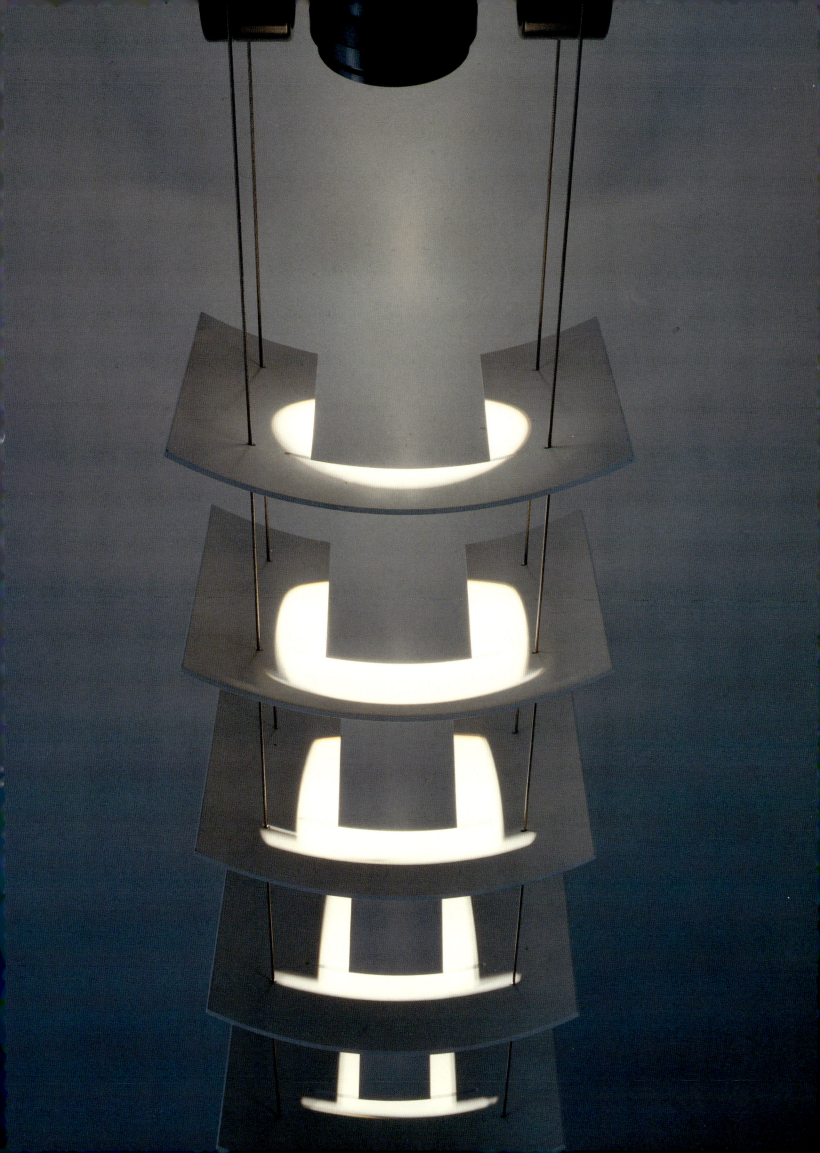

## Trio

**1988**
**Height 1000mm x Diameter 80mm**

Tiny, brightly colored acrylic diffusers add a happy spark to this set of halogen ceiling

pendants. Made of aluminum with a black finish, Trio was designed by Vladimir

Pezdirc, Ljubljana, Yugoslavia, and manufactured by Kvadrat, also of Ljubljana.

*Rock-It*

**1986**
**Rocks: Height 3¹/₂-5in x**
**Length 7-8in x Width 6-8in**
**Ceiling mount: Diameter 4¹/₂in x**
**Length 5¹/₂in**

With halogen fixtures inset into individual rocks that are suspended by aircraft cable from a ceiling-mounted transformer, Rock-It was designed and produced by Alex Mayer of Erna Treto Design, Washington, D.C.

## Squish

This series of three—a ceiling, sconce and suspension lamp—is made of transparent and frosted glass with a finely bevelled edge. The sconce and ceiling lamp are supported by a large button-shaped, painted metal disc, while the suspended version hangs by three wire cables and houses three halogen bulbs. Squish was designed by Fabio Di Bartolomei for Bieffeplast, Padova, Italy.

**1985**
Suspended lamp: Diameter 600mm;
Sconce: 250mm x 340mm x 100mm;
Ceiling lamp: Diameter 450mm x
Depth 140mm

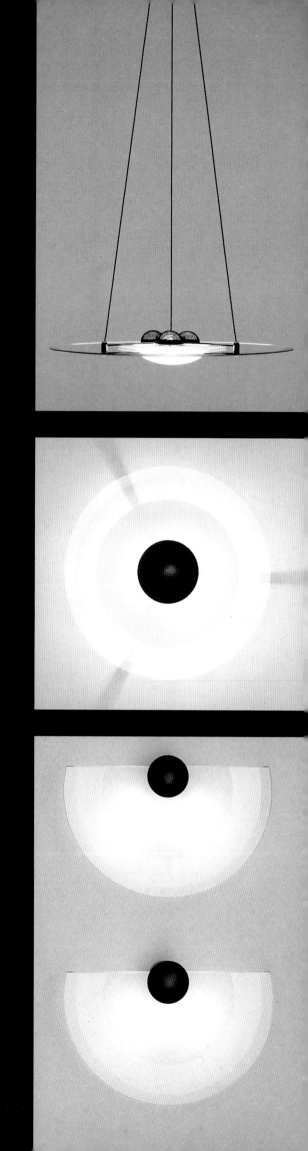

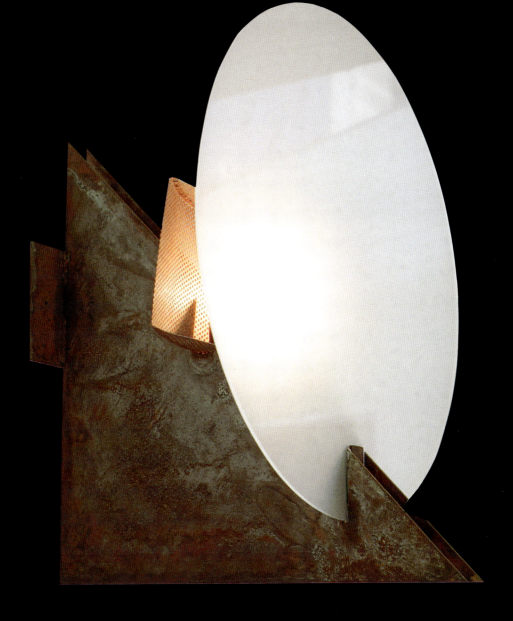

*Wall Sconce*

**1989**
**20in x 20in**

Made up of contrasting ele-

ments, this incandescent

Sini 1 is an incandescent desk lamp with an anodized aluminum dome shade and adjustable support. Designed by René Kemna of Imola, Italy, the lamp comes complete with an oversized on/off switch and Zamak base.

**1988**
**Base 270mm x Height 700mm**

## Grall

**1989**
Alpha: 77in x 42in;
Beta: 7.2in x 15.1in x 10.7in

Designed by Paolo Ferrari, Luciano Pagani and Angelo Perversi Associates for Flos Inc., Huntington Station, New York, the Grall lighting system comes in a number of adaptable models for contract or residential spaces. Grall Alpha, the floor version, has a scalloped frosted white or aquamarine glass diffuser secured by a cast aluminum alloy ringed support and balanced by a weighted humpbacked base. Grall Beta is a large scale sconce.

*Tulip*

**1987**
**22in x 13 ½in x 14in**

This organically shaped lighting fixture features an adjustable umbrella-like reflector that diffuses light in any direction. The lamp has a cast acrylic base, an aluminum body and arms, a phenolic baffle and a tough, closed cell extruded PVC reflector. A ring of 7-watt illumination circles the base to complement the major light source, a 75 watt halogen or incandescent lamp. Tulip was designed and manufactured by Ronald Reyburn, Ronald Reyburn Lighting Design, Long Beach, California.

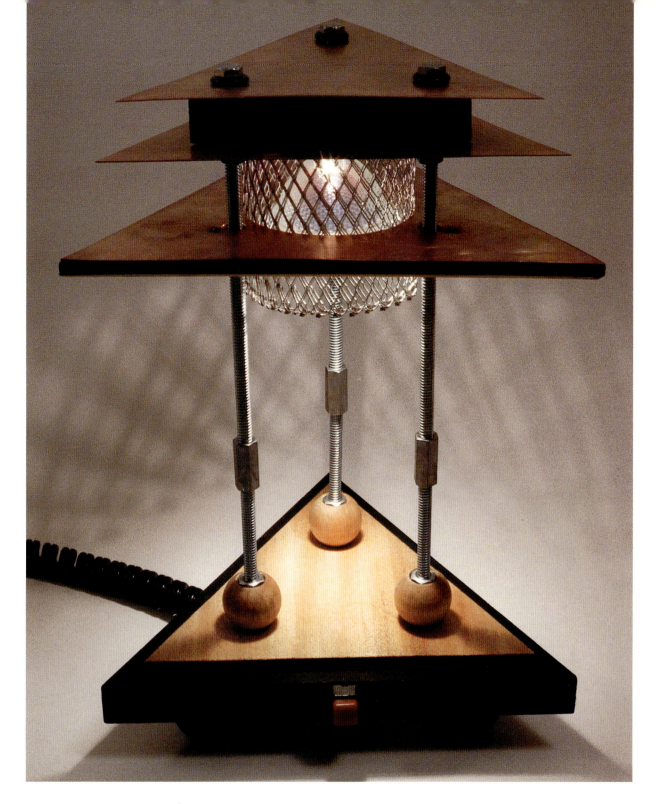

## Halogen Lamp

**1989**
**Height 12in x Width 8in x Depth 7 ½in**

Standing like a miniature monument, this table lamp is an intricate construction of wood, steel, and copper; its metal shade helps disperse the light. The light was designed and produced by Eric Margry of Eric Margry Design, Alexandria, Virginia.

## *A e To*

**1988**
**Floor Lamp:** 1970mm x 115mm;
**Sconce:** 480mm x 115mm

Looking like a large, watchful cat's eye. AeTo is a halogen sconce or floor lamp designed by Fabio Lombardo for Flos Inc., Huntington Station, New York, The lamp's swivelling reflector is made of varnished diecast aluminum; with a metallized glass diffuser; a varnished aluminum stem and a plastic base incorporated with a dimmer.

### Tris Tras

**1987**
**Diameter 19.7in x**
**Suspension height 7ft 5in**

Looking like a brightly glowing UFO, Tris Tras is made
up of an acrylic diffuser and
three tubular incandescent
lamps sandwiched between
two metal discs. This high-
tech ceiling fixture was designed by Perry A. King and
Santiago Miranda for Atelier
International Lighting, Long
Island City, New York.

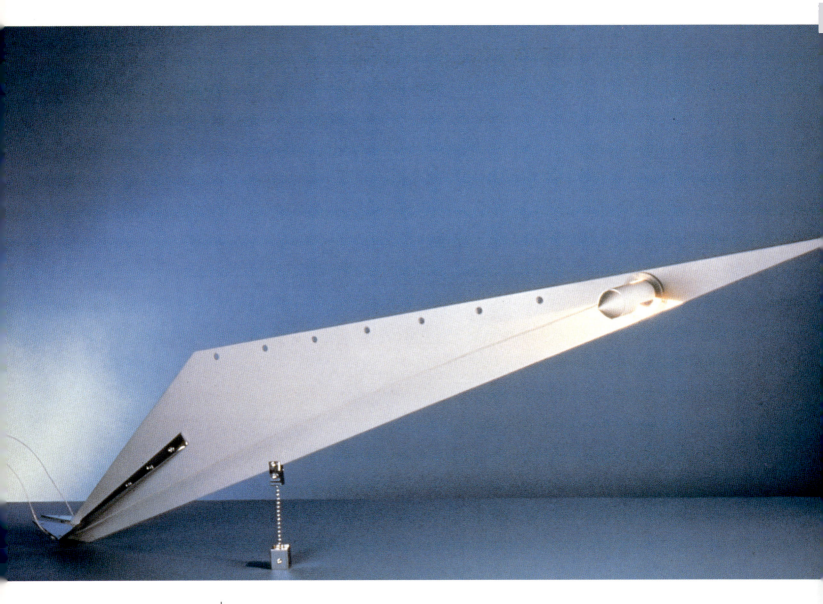

## Homage to Moholy Nagy

**1987**
**1800mm x 400mm**

Like a Constructivist work of art that dissects and repositions planes of light, Homage to Moholy Nagy is a halogen lamp that hangs from the ceiling, suspended as if about to take flight. Made of anodized sandblasted aluminum, the lamp was designed and produced by Studio Naço, Paris, France.

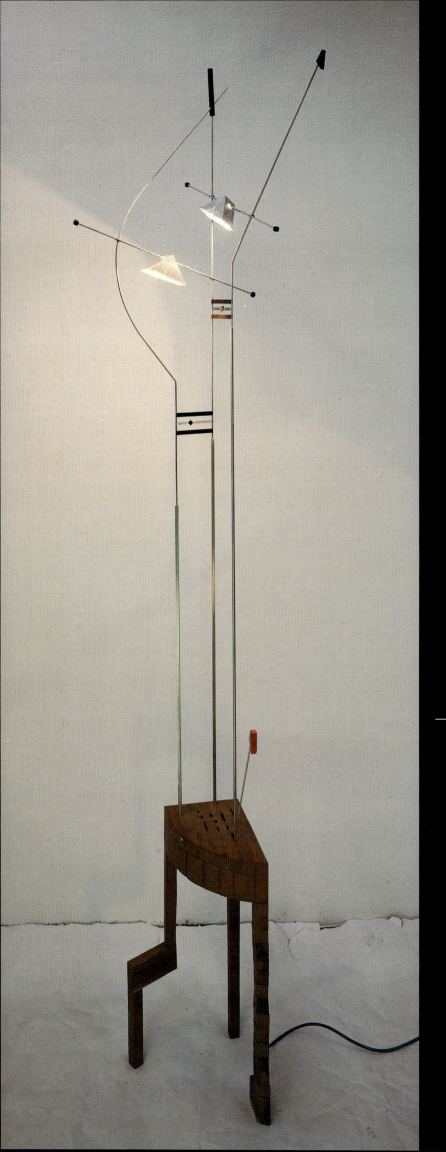

## *3 i*

**1987**
**Height 2150mm**

Made of slender aluminum rods that support three halogen light bulbs, and with a carved yew base, 3i was designed and fabricated by Thomas Eisl, London.

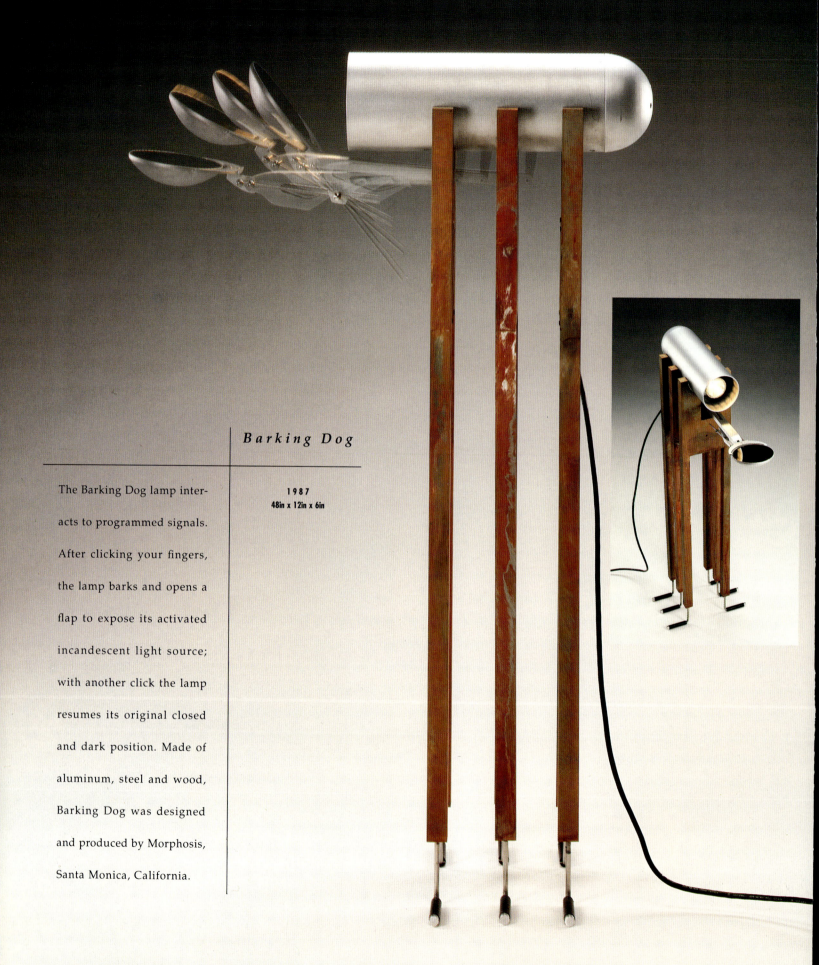

## *Barking Dog*

**1987**
**48in x 12in x 6in**

The Barking Dog lamp inter-

acts to programmed signals.

After clicking your fingers,

the lamp barks and opens a

flap to expose its activated

incandescent light source;

with another click the lamp

resumes its original closed

and dark position. Made of

aluminum, steel and wood,

Barking Dog was designed

and produced by Morphosis,

Santa Monica, California.

**1988**
**72in x 18in disc x 10in sphere**

With a weighted, cast resin ball resting in its base, Floor Lamp No.1 completely rotates on its axis and tilts 45 degrees from side to side. Designed and produced by Robert Silance of Clemson, South Carolina, the halogen floor lamp has a steel plate base, a stamped and extruded aluminum lamp housing and an etched plate glass diffuser.

## *Altair*

---

**1986**
Floor lamp: 1300mm; Table lamp: 400mm; Wall lamp: 350mm;
Ceiling lamp: Diameter 500mm x Arm length 300mm

This series of lamps for the wall, floor, desk or ceiling was designed and produced by Jorge Garcia Garay of Garcia Garay S.A., Barcelona, Spain. Minimal yet graceful, Altair is made of an exposed halogen bulb that easily pivots on its support bar to spread light in all directions. The base houses a transformer and energy is conducted straight to the light source by the structural wire frame. The ceiling version has two arms that swing 360 degrees and are positioned on the perimeter of a white epoxy disc reflecting indirect or direct light.

**1988**
71in x 10in x 10in

This nearly six-foot-tall bird-like lamp is constructed from cold rolled steel, stainless steel and water clear glass. The lamp's red incandescent light source is housed within bent perforated steel sheets tinged with rust, and its claw-like feet clutch at the cast concrete base. Dancing Angel was designed and produced by Morphosis, Santa Monica, California.

# ArenaVision

by Gerrit Arts

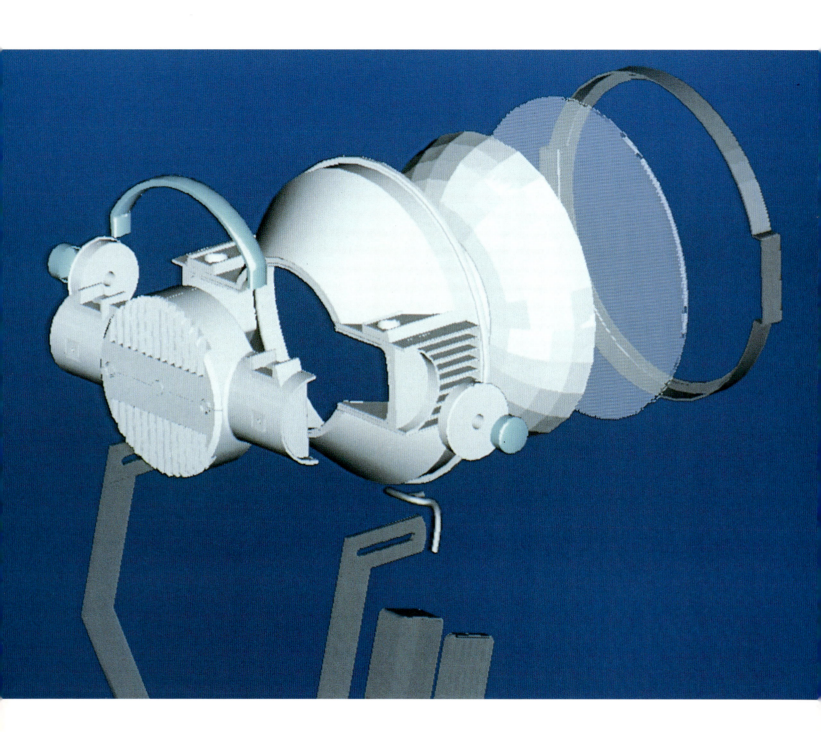

**1986**
**Diameter 475mm x Depth 238mm**

A lightweight high intensity floodlight, ArenaVision was designed to illuminate large to medium-sized stadia and indoor sports halls. Its compact robust form and easy to mount features allow architects to group the floodlights on mast frames or bank them on roof edges or in lighting galleries. Made of non-corrosive die-cast aluminum, the lamp's rear and front housings hinge open for maintenance and relamping; its sturdy blue die-cast grip allows workers to simply carry the unit in one hand. This precision lamp provides a well defined beam, reducing glare and light spill into areas surrounding the stadium. Its brilliant, natural colors make lighting better for the players in the arena, as well as for color TV reproduction. ArenaVision's principal designer was Gerrit Arts, with Robert Blaich, managing director of the corporate industrial design group and the CID lighting design team, Philips Lighting, Eindhoven, The Netherlands.

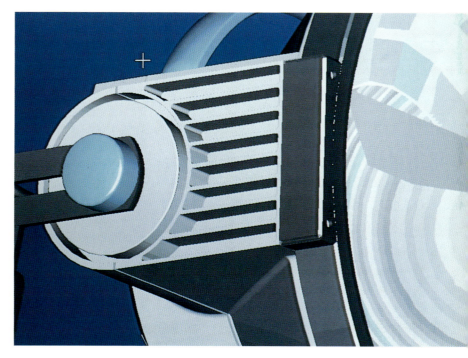

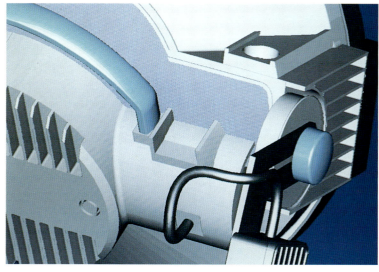

# Interview

*A graduate of the Academy of Industrial Design in Eindhoven, The Netherlands, Gerrit Arts has been a designer at Philips since 1951, and has designed lighting and luminaires since 1962. As part of the Philips Corporate Industrial Design (CID) team, Arts has received many awards for his work. An adjustable plug-in night light, professional plant irradiation luminaire and the ArenaVision Floodlight were all awarded the certificate of quality for good industrial design—IF Hanover. The ArenaVision also won an award in the 1989 ID Annual Design Review.*

**How was the project initiated?** The project was initiated in 1987 by Philips' Commercial Department. The idea was to develop a new sports light, replacing an earlier model designed in 1970. **How were you influenced or inspired?** For me, form still follows function, especially when designing professional products like the ArenaVision. Our first form studies, for example, were based on housing the 1800 W metal-halide lamp. In addition to drawings, foam models and computer-aided design, our technical department produced working models to test temperature, wind sensitivity, mechanics, production, access for maintenance and so on. All these factors influenced the design. **Did you use any special materials or technology?** A major design requirement was the use of lightweight yet robust components. The reflector and rear housing, for example, are made from non-corrosive aluminum; the entire floodlight weighs only 11 kilograms, considerably less than a conventional floodlight which weighs 18 kilograms. Floodlight mast installations are normally subject to 'drag' but the ArenaVision has a relatively small diameter of 445mm (a conventional diameter is 665mm), reducing wind loading by half. And since the ArenaVision is more efficient than conventional products in controlling light, fewer units are required to light sports activities. Fewer, smaller and lighter floodlights mean that the size of floodlight towers and head-frame structures can be reduced dramatically. **Does this lamp have any special function or purpose?** ArenaVision was specifically designed for lighting large to medium-sized stadia, for large indoor sports halls, and other facilities where high quality floodlighting is used. **Evaluate the success of your design.** Teamwork plus a new lamp plus new optics has created this updated design. **What would you like to design next?** Environmental light sculptures. **What is the future in lighting design?** Electronics will be integrated in lighting design, creating more intelligent products.

# Dinosaur II

**1988**
**Length 53³/₄in x Width 8³/₄in x Depth 10in**

Dinosaur II is a fluorescent lamp made of plexiglass sheets mounted one behind the other over the light source; light travels to the edge of the plexiglass, creating an eerie skeletal effect. This sculptural lamp was designed and produced by Pascal Luthi of Maison Dupin, Geneva, Switzerland.

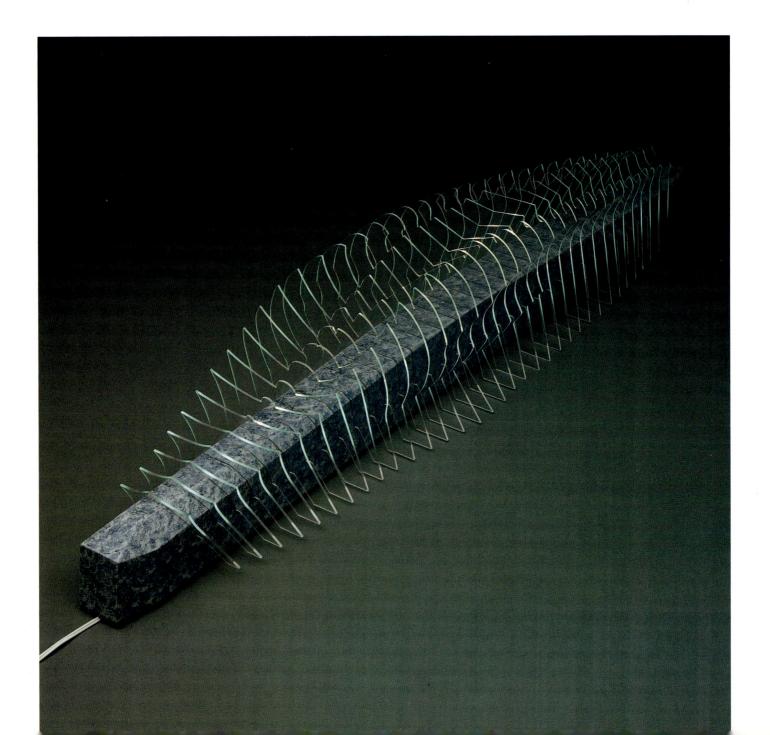

## *Eclipse Spotlight*

**1987**
**Width: 278mm x Max Length: 415mm x Depth 208mm**

Designed for exhibition halls and other large spaces where spotlighting is essential, the Eclipse Spotlight uses a high pressure discharge lamp to focus on objects and surfaces and, with the use of masks, to project logos, circles and patterns creating a number of special effects and moods. Eclipse is a complete system that integrates a basic aluminum housing with a choice of special light heads and clip-on accessories, including color filters, infra-red reflectors and UV filters. The spotlight was designed by Mario Bellini, Milan Italy, and manufactured byErco Leuchten GmbH, Ludenscheid, West Germany.

*Rinascimento*

**1988**
**Height 620mm x Diameter 210 mm**

This simple, elegant halogen desk lamp, with its softly curved traditional forms, is made of engraved and sanded pearly glass. Rinascimento was designed by Matteo Thun of Thun Associates, Milan, and manufactured by Barovier E Toso, Munaro, Italy.

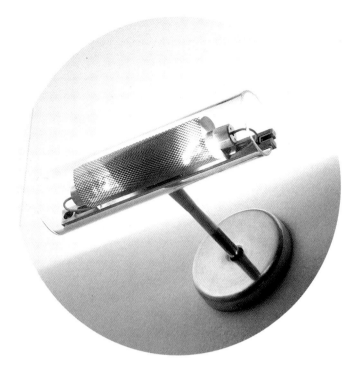

## Acheo

**1989**
**Floor lamp: 1810mm x 300mm;**
**Wall lamp: 235mm x 210mm**

Designed by Gianfranco Frattini, Milan, Italy, the Acheo floor and wall lamp both have a metal stem and base with a metallic grey lacquer finish. A clear pyrex glass diffuser is mounted on a die-cast aluminum support, and the floor lamp has adjustable tension cables made of clear plastic-coated steel with black rubber elastic terminals. The halogen lamps are manufactured by Artemide S.p.A., Milan.

## *Bali*

An incandescent or fluorescent wall sconce, Bali was designed by Luciano Pagani for Atelier International Lighting, Long Island City, New York. Supported by triangular shaped tubular arms, the sconce's distinctive opal glass diffuser can be pivoted in a variety of positions.

**1988**
Width 12in x Height 17in x Depth 9.5in - 13in (adjustable)

## Ms. Dee Dee Deluxe

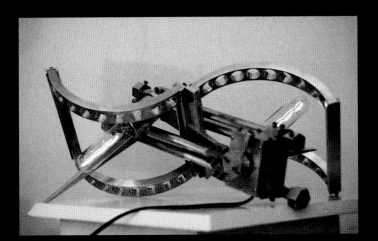

**1988**
**26in x 10in x 10in**

Using what looks like pieces of scrap metal, alminum bars and tubing, stainless steel screws and bolts, this sculptural lamp can either stand or recline and incoporates two six-inch incandescent bulbs; its dimmer is built into a metal box. Ms. Dee Dee Deluxe was designed and produced by David Gale of the Gallery of Functional Art, Santa Monica, California.

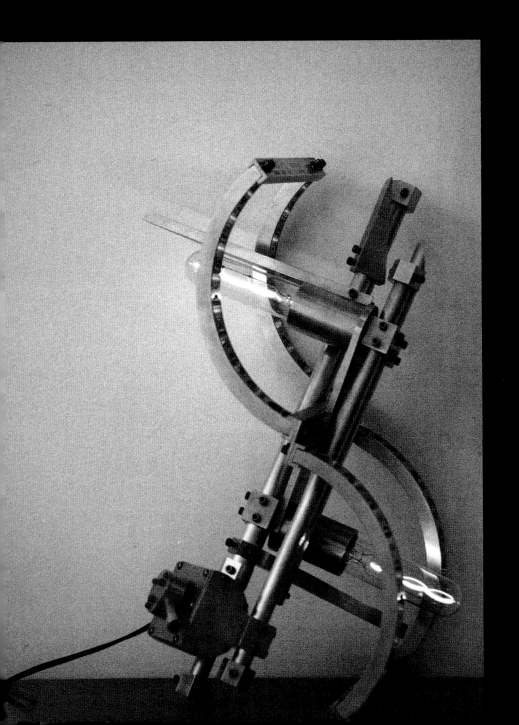

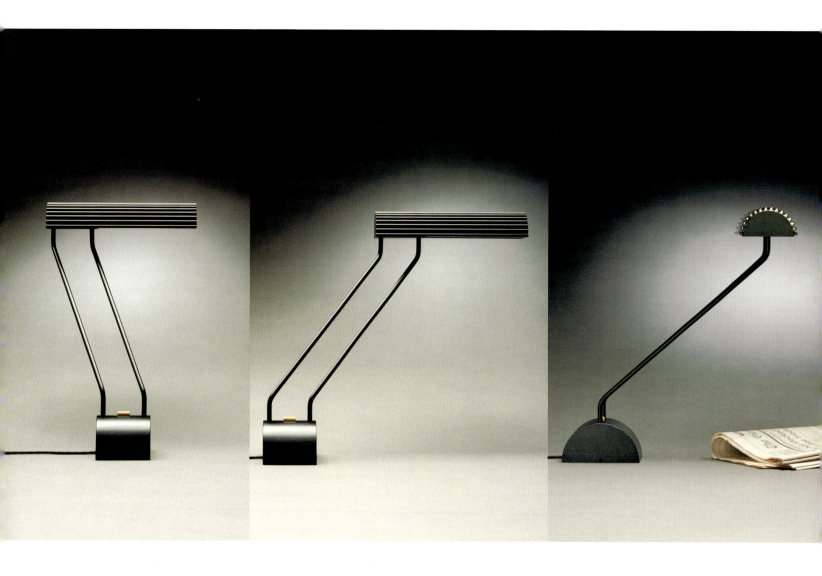

## Pantograph

### 1988
**Height: 15in  Reflector: 10¼in x 3in**

With a PL-13 fluorescent light source, sandcasted base, stainless steel supports and an extruded aluminum reflector, the Pantograph desk lamp was designed in-house by Michel Dallaire of Michel Dallaire Designers Inc., Montreal, Canada. The lamp articulates horizontally 160 degrees by means of a pantograph mechanism.

The Halo-Click Light System incorporates three distinct design elements: a chunky cube or cylindrical base, a long graceful tubular neck and a rotating cylindrical reflector. The combination of elements depends on whether the lamp is designed for wall, floor, track or table. Made of polycarbonate, the lamps were designed by Sottsass Associati, Milan, Italy, for Philips Italia, also of Milan.

## *Aerial Light*

Aerial Light, a wild assembly of cast metal wires, is operated by infra-red remote control. The lamp swivels and tilts in a multitude of directions and its aerial stem can be extended to a maximum of 1300mm. This halogen desk or table lamp was designed and produced by Ron Arad of One Off Ltd., London, England.

**1987**
Height 300mm to 1300mm
Diameter 200mm x

## Eco

### 1988
**Floor lamp:** Height 1320mm to 1910mm;
**Wall lamp:** Extension
530mm; **Ceiling lamp:** Height 600mm x
Extension 1280mm

With geometric grace, the Eco halogen lights swivel and tilt, directing light in all directions. Designed for the wall, ceiling and floor, the lamps are made from anodized aluminum and plastic and come in either black or white. Eco was designed by Mario Barbaglia and Marco Colombo for Paf, Milan, Italy and is distributed in the U.S. by Koch + Lowy, Long Island City, New York.

## El Globo

**1985**
**480mm x 530mm x 290mm**

This table lamp allows light to revolve freely on its axis above a solid marble base. A 12-volt current is conducted by the lamp's nickeled steel supports to power the halogen light source. El Globo was designed by Studio Naço, Paris, France, and is produced by Lucien Gau, also of Paris.

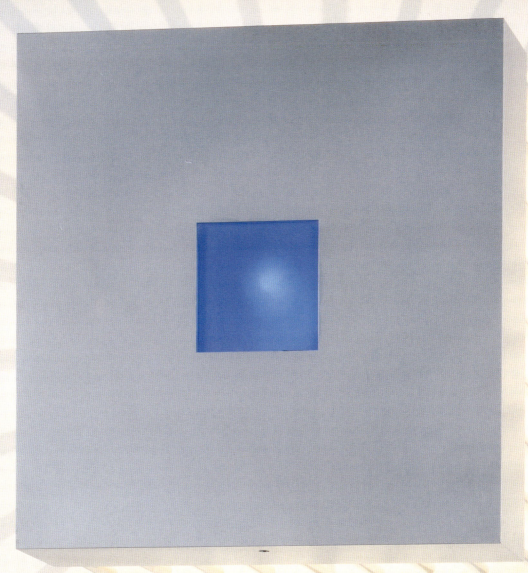

## Chip Wall Sconce

**1988**
**8in x 8in x 4in**

Designed and produced in-house by Piotr Sierakowski of Koch + Lowy, Long Island City, New York, this dramatic wall sconce encases its halogen light source within a distinctive aluminum box. White light bursts through gaps made by a series of small stainless steel poles that set the light off from the wall; light also shines through the center accent of cobalt-blue glass.

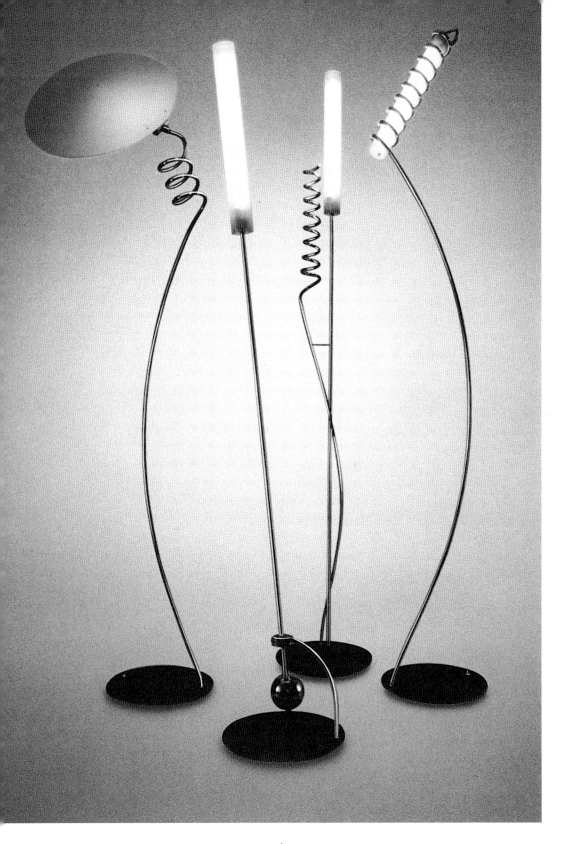

## Night Shades

**1987**
**1800mm x 350mm**

Inspired by the twisted, spiralled forms of its name sake, a poisonous climbing plant, Nightshades is a collection of stainless steel floor lamps designed by Ulrich Hoereth of N16 Projectanentur, Vienna, Austria, and manufactured by Woka Lamps, also of Vienna. Each fixture has a steel stem supporting a fluorescent tube, while ball and socket joints allow the lamps to tip and swing.

## Lippa

**1985**
Lippa/Parete-Sofitto:
Height 350, 550 or 750mm x
Length 360 mm x
Width 245 mm; Lippa/Salisce:
Height 3500mm x
Length 500mm x Width 245mm;
Lippa/Cavalletto:
Height 1740mm x Length 500mm.

With special mounting supports for wall, floor or ceiling, Lippa is a die-cast aluminum lamp that revolves freely, like a spindle, on its horizontal access; a pair of adjustable lateral diffusing flaps precisely direct the light. Lippa was designed by Maurizio Bertoni, Milan, Italy, and manufactured by Castaldi Illuminazione S.p.A., also of Milan.

## *Floor Lamp No.2*

**1989**
**72in x 18in**

Designed and produced by Robert Silance of Clemson, South Carolina, Floor Lamp No. 2 has an etched glass diffuser and an anodized aluminum channel that acts as the vertical support, lamp housing and powercord raceway.

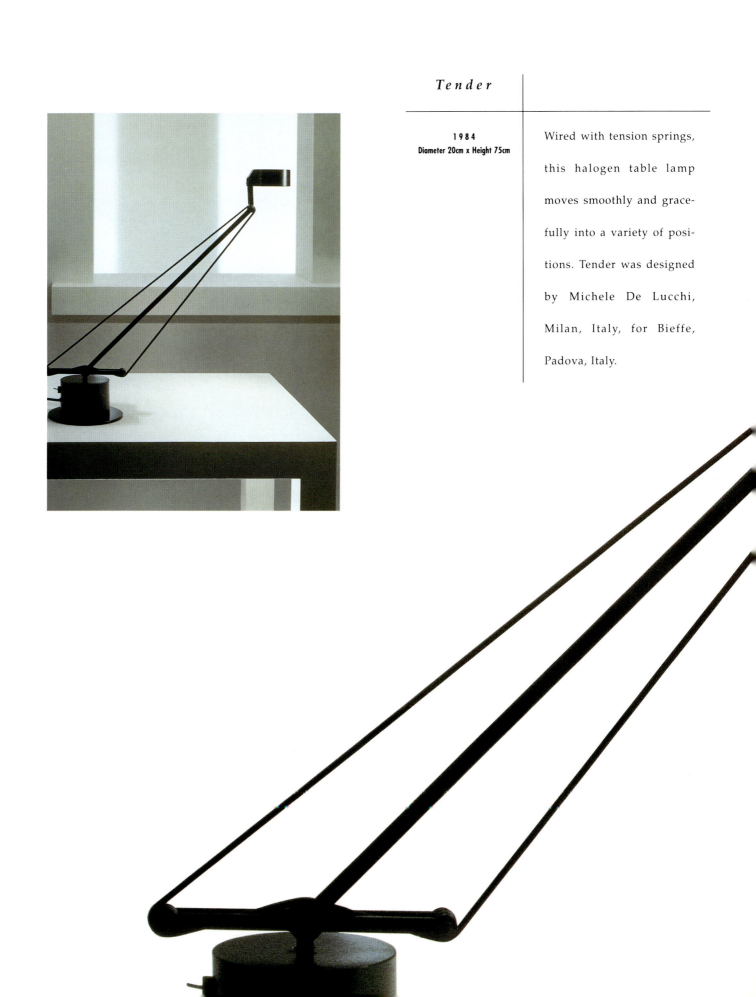

## Tender

**1984**
**Diameter 20cm x Height 75cm**

Wired with tension springs, this halogen table lamp moves smoothly and gracefully into a variety of positions. Tender was designed by Michele De Lucchi, Milan, Italy, for Bieffe, Padova, Italy.

*terprise*

by Jorge Garcia Garay

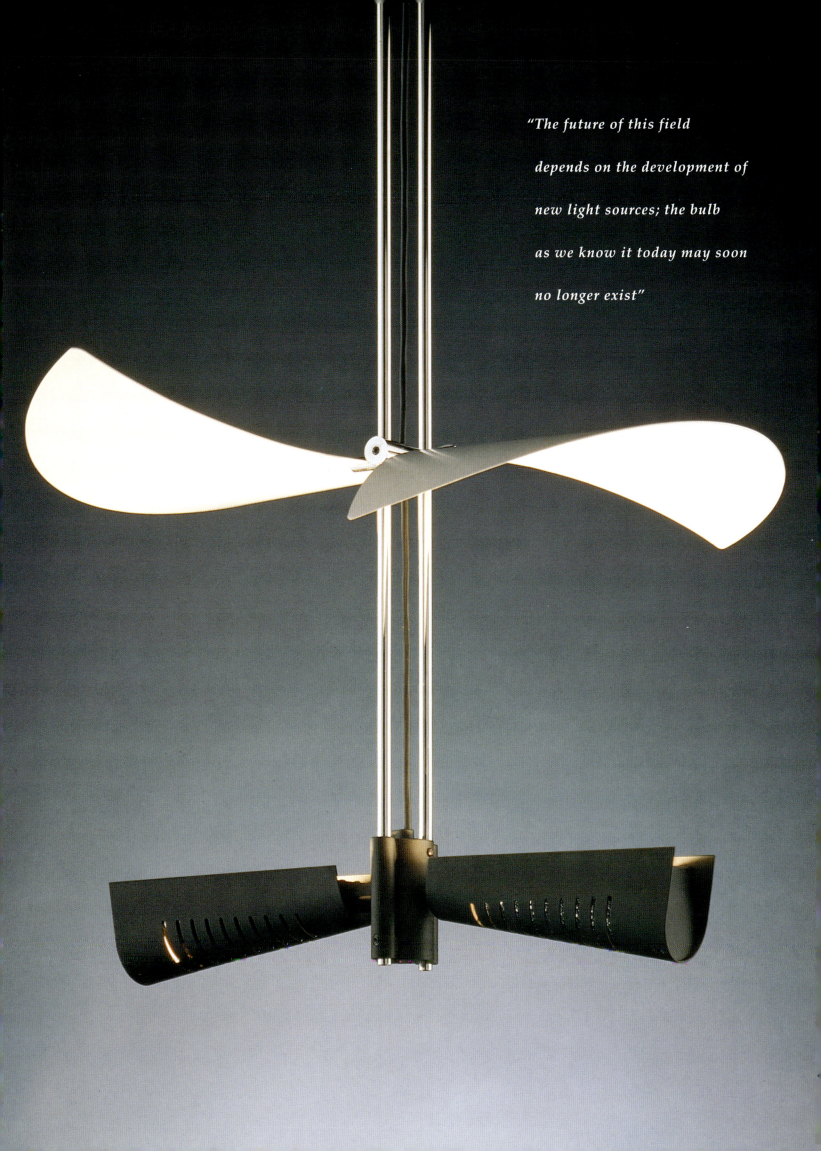

*"The future of this field depends on the development of new light sources; the bulb as we know it today may soon no longer exist"*

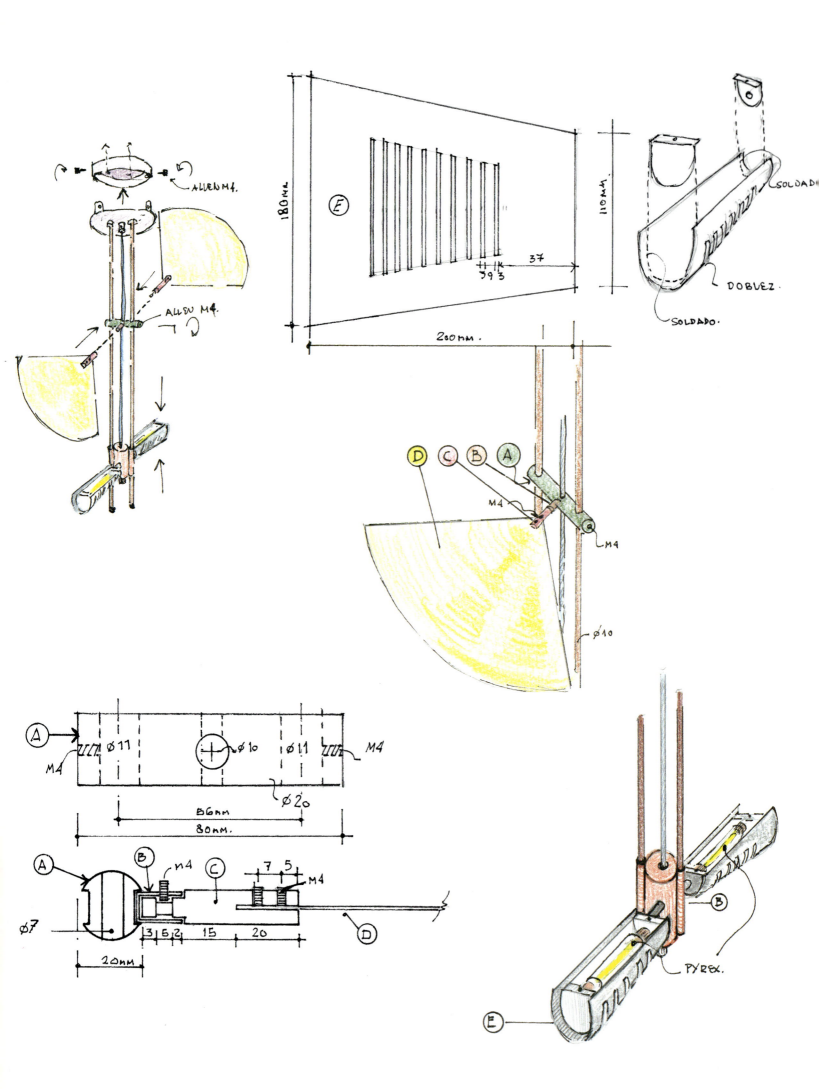

ALLEN M4.

ALLEN M4.

E

180mm

110mm

37

393

200mm.

SOLDADO

DOBLEZ.

SOLDADO.

D C B A

M4

M4

⌀10

A

M4

⌀11

⌀10

⌀11

M4

M4

⌀20

56mm

80mm.

A

B

m4

C

7 5

M4

⌀7

D

3 5 2

15

20

20mm

PYREX.

E

B

## Enterprise

**1988**
**Ceiling lamp: Width 500mm;**
**Floor lamp: Height 200mm x**
**Width 250mm with one focus**
**or 500mm with two;**
**Sconce: Height 250mm x**
**Width 250mm**

Versatile and elegantly proportioned, the three versions of Enterprise, a floor lamp, a hanging lamp and a sconce, exhibit a striking mastery of style and craft. Although their configurations vary, the lamp's basic elements remain the same: two parallel metal rods as the support structure, white metal or epoxy fan blades as reflectors, and either one or two trapeze shaped focus mechanisms that house the halogen light source and aluminum shade. The fans and focus mechanisms can be positioned up and down the rods and rotate freely through 360 degrees to softly spread light around the room for different lighting functions. Enterprise was designed and produced by Garcia Garay S.A. in Barcelona, Spain.

# Interview

*A licensed architect in Buenos Aires, Argentina, Jorge Garcia Garay now works in the production and design of lighting and furniture in Barcelona, Spain. His designs have received numerous awards and have been exhibited in museums around the world. The Enterprise lamps were part of the 1989 opening exhibition of the Design Museum in London*

**How were you influenced or inspired?** To explain how the Enterprise lights evolved I must go back to the first project where I used reflected light. This lamp was called Urania and was conceived as an all-geometric object. It was a triangular structure with a circular base and white spherical diffuser. For my next project I used even stronger geometrical elements but its feeling was more spatial. Here I came up with the idea of aerodynamic reflecting foils. **Did you use any special materials or technology?** The lamp is simply made of two metal tubes along which are a focus mechanism (which houses the halogen light source) and reflector fan blades made of white epoxy or metal. The focus and fan move up and down the tubes and are fixed at the desired height with an allen key. **What was the biggest obstacle?** The biggest obstacle was regulating the heat produced by the transformer. Rectangular holes in the metal focus shade create some ventilation. **What alternatives were explored?** At first the reflector fans were flat and did not revolve. All they could do was slide up and down the tubes. While testing them with the source of light, I decided that they needed to be slightly round and should rotate 360 degrees to reflect light at any angle. The next step was to design the focus mechanisms. Their trapeze shape gives them enough roundness to house the halogen bulb and aluminum shade. **What would you like to design next?** A lamp with an arm that swings like a metronome that would provide specific light for reading. **What is the future of lighting design?** In the past few years there has been a revolution in lighting design. The advent of the halogen bulb for domestic use, for example, has made lighting much more subtle and aerial. The future depends on the development of new light sources. Where the bulb as we know it today may no longer exist, we may be designing with electro-luminescent light panels or optic fibers. This may all seem like it's out of a science fiction movie but the technology exists.

## Table Lamp

**1989**
12in x 18in x 2½in

This simple and functional table lamp was designed by Kirti Trivedi and K. Munshi of the Industrial Design Center, Bombay, India and manufactured by the Design Cell, also of Bombay. Red and blue electrical connecting wires weave in zig-zags through a transparent acrylic sheet to connect the lamp base and reflector.

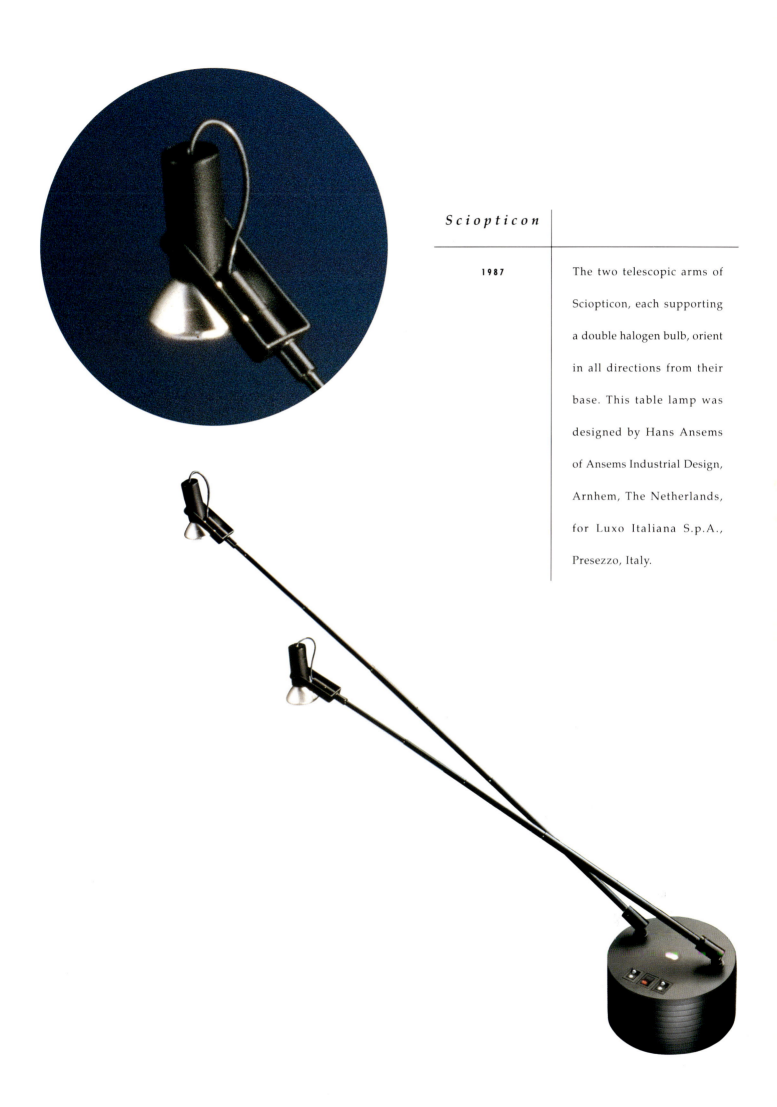

## Sciopticon

**1987**

The two telescopic arms of Sciopticon, each supporting a double halogen bulb, orient in all directions from their base. This table lamp was designed by Hans Ansems of Ansems Industrial Design, Arnhem, The Netherlands, for Luxo Italiana S.p.A., Presezzo, Italy.

## Guardian Lamps

**1987**
**48in x 24in x 18in**

Designed and produced by Robly A. Glover Jr., Bloomington, Indiana, the Guardian lamps are full of character and movement. Like a spindly, long-legged stick figure, the lamp is made of brass and copper chemically treated with patina to produce a green-blue surface. Halogen lamps housed behind a circular and a triangular shade, cast patterns of light against the wall and floor.

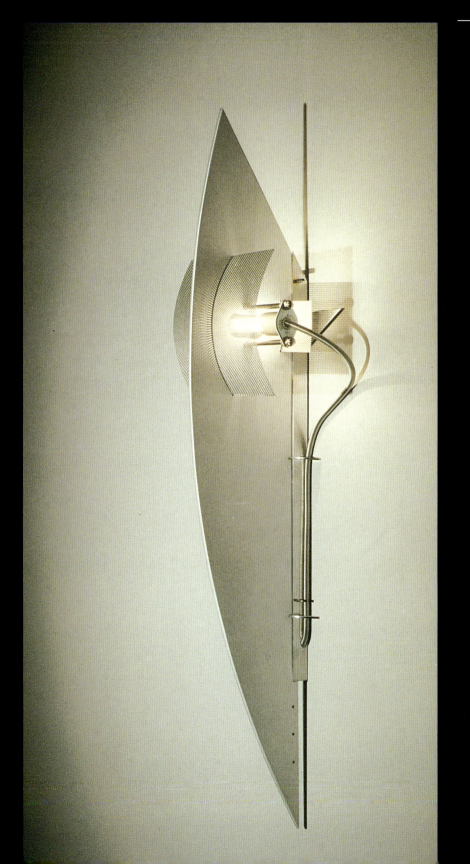

## Squale

**1988**
590mm x 120mm x 150mm

The designers of Studio Naço, Paris, France, wanted to create an "animalistic" object as a source of light. This sconce, therefore, has a sharp aluminum blade pierced by the halogen light source as its centerpiece, with an inverted reflector hovering at the top of the conductive wire like the head of a serpent. Made of anodized aluminum and stainless steel, Squale is manufactured by Lucien Gau, Paris, France.

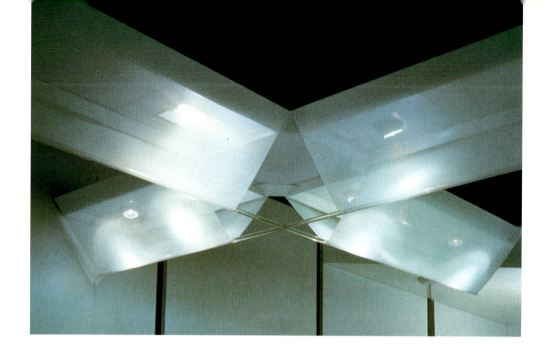

*Soffio*

1987

An overhead track-lighting system, Soffio accomodates both high and low voltage lighting; the same lighting tray supports fluorescent tubes that can be combined and interchanged with halogen or filament bulbs. Made of extuded aluminum and shaded with woven polypropylene mesh, the lighting system was designed by Emilio Ambasz, New York, for Sirrah S.p.A., Imola, Italy.

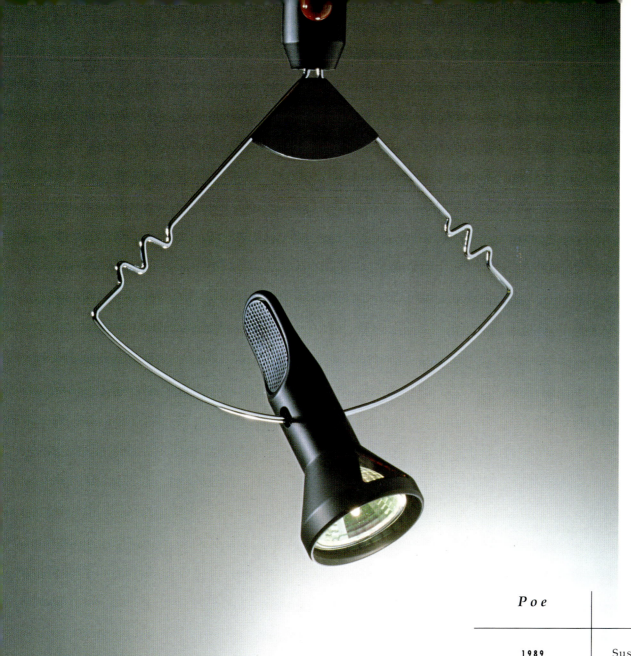

## Poe

**1 9 8 9**
**295mm x 260mm**

Suspended on what looks like an arc of electrical current, Poe is a low-voltage dichroic modular spotlight system that can be ceiling-, wall- or track-mounted. The spotlight, which pivots on a chrome support, is made of die-cast aluminum with a light grey or matt black finish. Poe was designed by Giugiaro Design, Turin, Italy, and manufactured by Luci S.p.A., Milan, Italy.

### SB-16
### Spacebird

**1989**
**Height 8 1/2in x Depth 2 3/4in**

An invigorated twist to track lighting, the SB-16 Spacebird series is constructed of lightweight extruded aluminum coated in black, white or silver high-temperature paint. Adjustable and self-locking, both horizontally and vertically, Spacebird's sculptural shape helps to transmit light in all directions. Designed in-house by Kenneth Kane of Lighting Services Inc., Stony Point, New York, the halogen fixture can be mounted on the ceiling or wall.

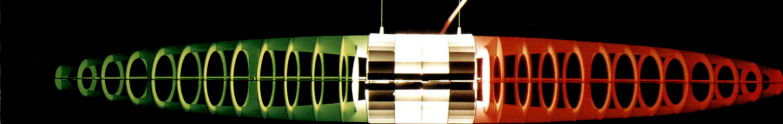

*Titania*

1989

Like a computer rendering of a three dimensional ellipse illuminated with bright iridescent colors, Titania is a halogen lamp suspended from the ceiling by steel cables. With a lamellar metal envelope that screens and reflects the halogen light, the lamp's extended elliptical shape is made of mill finished anodized aluminum blades. Interchangeable color filters of silk screened polycarbonate sheeting create magnificent lighting effects. Titania was designed by Alberto Meda and Paolo Rizzatto for Luceplan, Milan, Italy.

### Star

**1987**
**Height 40in - 80in x Width 5 ¹/₂in**

A small-scale, low-voltage series of pendant fixtures, Star provides down and reflected light through its conic hand-blown Murano glass diffuser with tranlucent glass trim. The lamp was designed by Roberto Pamio of Leucos, Venice, Italy, and distributed in the United States by IPI Lighting, Long Island City, New York.

## "Uchida" Lamp

**1987**
72in x 16in x 16in

Using spartan elements—a simple grey tripod support and a square sheet mesh—designer Shigeru Uchida of Studio 80, Tokyo, Japan, created an expressive floor lamp that transmits magnificent patterns of gridded light on the ceiling and walls. The Uchida Lamp is manufactured by Studio 80 and distributed in the United States by Gallery 91, New York.

**1986**
**Height 14in x Length 17in**

The Lucy and Tania lamps were designed by Harvey J. Mackie of Colorado in London, England. With twin plexiglass halos positioned over two naked incandescent globes, the lamps are supported by clear plexiglass rods on a black lacquered base.

*M a s k*

**1989**
**12in x 16in**

With a Tyvek paper shade gently retained by wire shaped in an elliptical loop, Mask is an incandescent table lamp designed and fabricated by David Potter of David Potter Industrial Design, Los Angeles, California.

## Picchio

**1984**
**670mm**

This collection of brightly colored plastic table lamps were designed by Isao Hosoe,

Milan, Italy, and were manufactured by Luxo Italiana, S.p.A. Presezzo, Italy. The lamp-

head, which houses a flourescent tube, directs light on three different planes.

## SL48 Solar Lantern

**1987**
22in x 13³/₄in x 3⁵/₈in

A self-contained rechargeable light source for use in remote locations, the Solar Lantern converts sunlight into electricity, charging its internal battery through solar cells placed on one side. Its other side houses a fluorescent tube that emits a 40-watt light for up to four hours. The lantern, made of injection molded clear fire-retardent polycarbonate, was designed by Hedda Beese and Charles Ash of Moggridge Associates, London, England, and manufactured by BP Solar International, Aylesbury, Bucks, England.

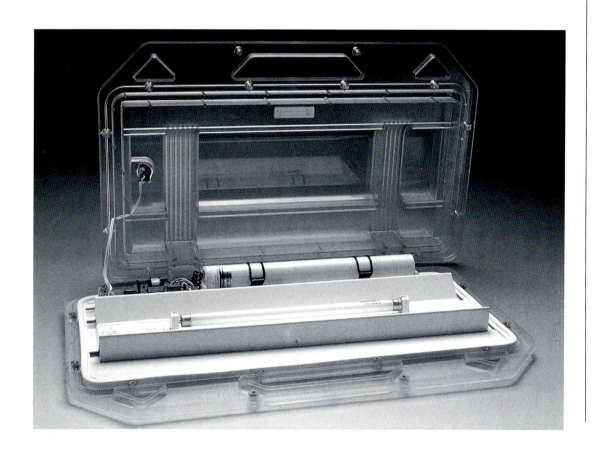

_China_

1989

Designed as a compromise between two generics, the black mechanical task lamp and the traditional brass banker's lamp, China provides direct dual intensity light. The lamp has a spun aluminum reflector finished in white baked enamel and a metallic red or anthracite baked enamel cap. Its supporting stem is made of brushed stainless steel with an elliptical cross section. With a cast-iron base and a stem support finished in silver enamel, China is manufactured by Atelier International Lighting, Long Island City, New York, and was designed in-house by Stephan Copeland.

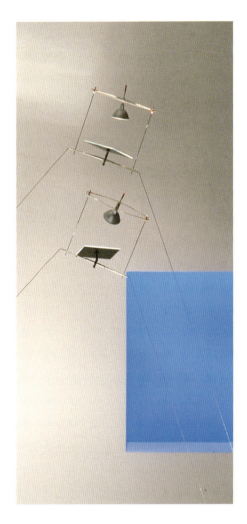

## Ya Ya Ho

**1984**
**216in average wire span**

YaYaHo is a conglomeration of transformer, cables and various lighting elements that dangle in the air like skybound jewelry. Designed in-house by Ingo Maurer and team, Munich, West Germany, this ceramic, glass, plastic, metal and porcelain fixture allows its user a measure of artistic freedom; all horizontal and some vertical parts are movable, and all lighting elements can be repositioned on the cables.

Focus on:

*de Down*

by Jan Van Lierde

"*People should not only decide how long or how high their environment is; they should also decide its visual aspect, its total atmosphere.*"

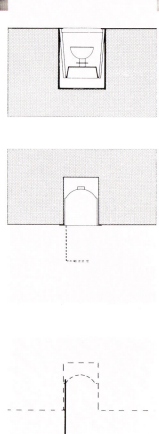

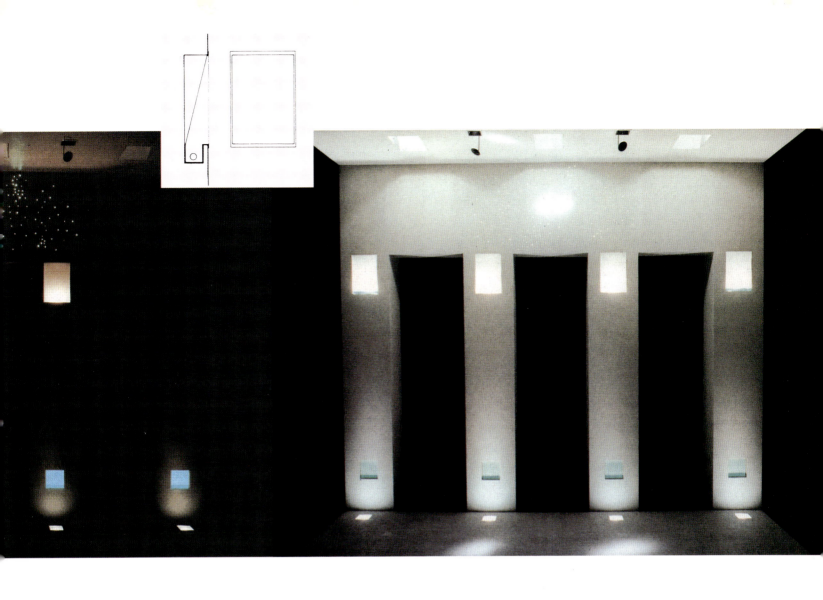

## Upside Down

This series of up, side and down lighting integrates to illuminate the complete interior. Made up of neat cubes inset into the wall, ceiling and floor, each lighting fixture has a name that refers to the way it projects light. Side, for example, is a recessed assembly box for all side lighting and houses incandescent, flourescent, halogen or metal halide bulbs. Down is a ceiling super spotlight whose housing is made of 0.04 inch thick sheet steel; it has an optional color filtered mirror to redirect the light. Up, a waterproof floor spotlight, has a polished cast aluminum housing that incorporates a universal lampholder and heatproof glass cover. Out has a polished cast aluminum assembly plate and a frame that houses white, green or blue electroluminescent panels for night lighting, security, pictograpms and graphics. Upside Down was designed by Jan Van Lierde, Kreon N.V., Antwerp, Belgium, and is distributed in the United States by the Modern Age Gallery, New York.

# Interview

*After attending Jesuit College in Belgium for three years, Jan Van Lierde quit to study architecture at Shias in Gent, Belgium. Graduating in 1978, Van Lierde started his own architectural practice, working on private housing and factories in Belgium, Egypt, Algeria, Italy and Scotland. At the same time, he founded Kreon in Antwerp, a company that represents European artists and designers, buys and sells contemporary lighting and consults on special lighting projects.*

**How was the project initiated?** After years of consulting on lighting, we started a department at Kreon to manufacture decorative luminaires. As our production facilities became more sophisticated we decided to enter the field of contract lighting with a special project line that we could produce ourselves. **How were you influenced?** As an architect I developed a style that considers and analyses human needs. I wanted to reflect these needs, and a way of life, in abstract spaces with a minimum of decorative elements so that the environment is both free from things and free for things. The fixture itself is not so important, but the effect you get from it is. I wanted to create an effect so that when people walk into a space they like it but are not sure why. **Did you use any special materials or technology?** We wanted to integrate technically advanced lighting products. We used fluorescent, halogen, incandescent and metal halide lamps and electroluminescent lighting panels. **Evaluate the success of your design.** We do not look at what the whole world is doing in design. We try to make our own decisions and we have our own way of acting. We have come up with something completely different in contract lighting without resorting to track lighting and without getting too complicated. We try to be fresh and young, to design with freedom, and that maybe is the answer to our success. **What would you like to design next?** We would like to create a lighting gift that stimulates other senses. When you enter a space it has its own character; we are working on an idea that allows people to identify with their environment, to make it personally theirs through the use of light. We have five senses and with light we only use one or two, sight and sometimes touch. We want to bring another sense to lighting. **What is the future of lighting design?** Lighting should become a fourth dimension. People should not only decide how long or how high their space or environment is, they should also decide the visual aspect, the total atmosphere. People are now more aware of their environment and light plays a big part.

# *Quahog*

**1986**
**Height 72in x Width 7 ¹/₂in x Depth 8in**

Quahog, a halogen floor lamp, has a bellow-shaped rice paper shade and a brushed aluminum armature. Looking like a fluted white clamshell, the lamp shade electronically unfolds, operated by a switch that simultaneously controls the brightness of the bulb. Quahog was designed and produced by Leo Blackman and Lance Chantry of Immaculate Concepts, New York.

*Luna*

**1986**
**Diameter 600mm**

Beautifully crafted, Luna, a halogen lamp, gracefully suspends from the ceiling. A frosted-blue crystal disc absorbs and diffuses light reflected from the spotlight housed within its spun aluminum shade. The luminaire was designed in-house by Josep Llusca, Blauet S.A., Barcelona, Spain.

## Victory

Designed by De Pas, D'Urbino and Lomazzi, Milan, Italy, Victory is a floor, wall or extensible wall lamp with a laquered metal support structure and a shell-like china diffuser that houses a halogen bulb. Victory is manufactured by Stilnovo, also of Milan.

1989

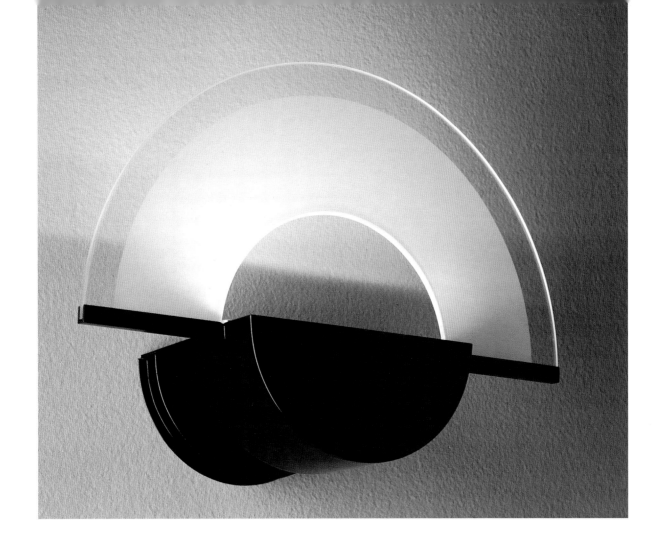

### *Ares*

**1986**
**Floor lamp: 300mm x 1940mm;**
**Sconce: 140mm x 360mm**
**x 140mm**

Casting a soft glow of light from its semi-circular glazed demiline diffuser, the Ares floor lamp and sconce was designed by Roberto Marcatti of Lavori in Corso, Milan, Italy, and is part of the Zeus Collection, manufactured by Noto SRL, also of Milan. The lamps' supports are made of die-cast aluminum finished in black epoxy.

## Pendant

**1987**
**Diameter 20in x Length 32in**

With a translucent acrylic sheet laminated between two circular black panels, the Pendant ceiling lamp transmits down light from its halogen source and radiates, with the use of fibre optics, a thin line of blue or red around its perimeter. The lamp was designed in-house by Frederick Ramond Inc., Cerritos, California.

## *Urushi*

**1986**
**Height 655mm x Width 345mm x Depth 215mm**

Urushi, a small floor lamp, is made of lacquered wood and special Japanese paper.

The designer, Toshiyuki Kita of IDK Design Laboratory Ltd., Osaka, Japan, has created

a gentle balance between traditional Japanese craftsmanship and contempoary design.

The lamp is manufactured by Omukaikosyudo, Wajma Ishikawa, Japan.

## Orbit

**1987**
**Diameter 75mm x Length 60mm**

A program of small, compact 12-volt halogen spotlights, Orbit, made of die-cast aluminum, can either be track- or ceillng-mounted. The system was designed by Peter Krouwel of Ninaber/Peters/Krouwel, Delft, The Netherlands.

## Lester 220

**1987**
**Height 800mm x Length 1000mm**

Sleek and minimal, this lacquered aluminum desk lamp was designed by Vico Magistretti, Milan, Italy, and manufactured by Oluce, also of Milan. Its base and reflector, both finished in black nextel, remain horizontal as they are adjusted. The lamp's arm rotates 360 degrees at the base and the pivot support cuts sharp angles as it moves.

## *P i*

**1 9 8 7**
**75in x 21in**

A six-foot interpretation of
the transcendental number
after which it was named, Pi
is a tubular-steel floor lamp
designed and produced by
Jan Van Lierde of Kreon
N.V., Antwerp, Belgium. The
lamp is distributed in the
United States by the Modern
Age Gallery, New York.

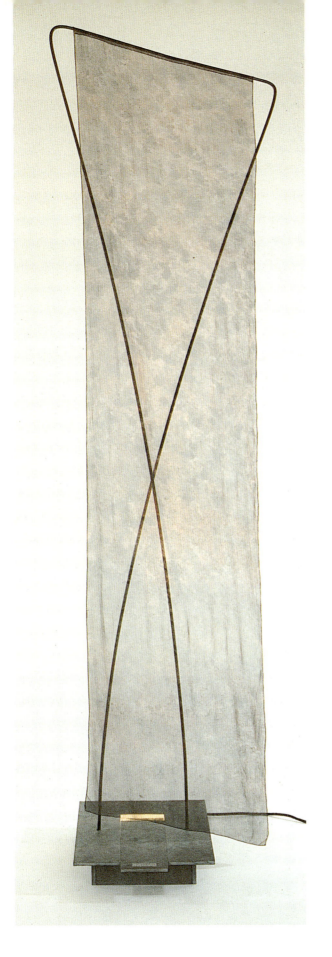

**1988**
80in x 20in x 18in

This sculptural floor lamp, designed by Mark Parrish, Brooklyn New York, tor Art et Industrie, New York has a stone base stabilizing its tall, wispy steel frame. Draped in silk chiffon, the lamp's halogen source shines upward from the base, reflecting light through the graceful length of sheer fabric; a micro-switch within the base adjusts the intensity and direction of light.

**1988**
80in x 20in x 18in

## Hanger

1987
10in x 8in x 8in

This table lamp is made of the simplest of materials—sheets of white paper and wire coat hangers. Diffusing soft incandescent light through the paper's folds, the lamp stands on three tiny acrylic feet and was designed and produced by Michael Pinkus of Pinkus Design, New York.

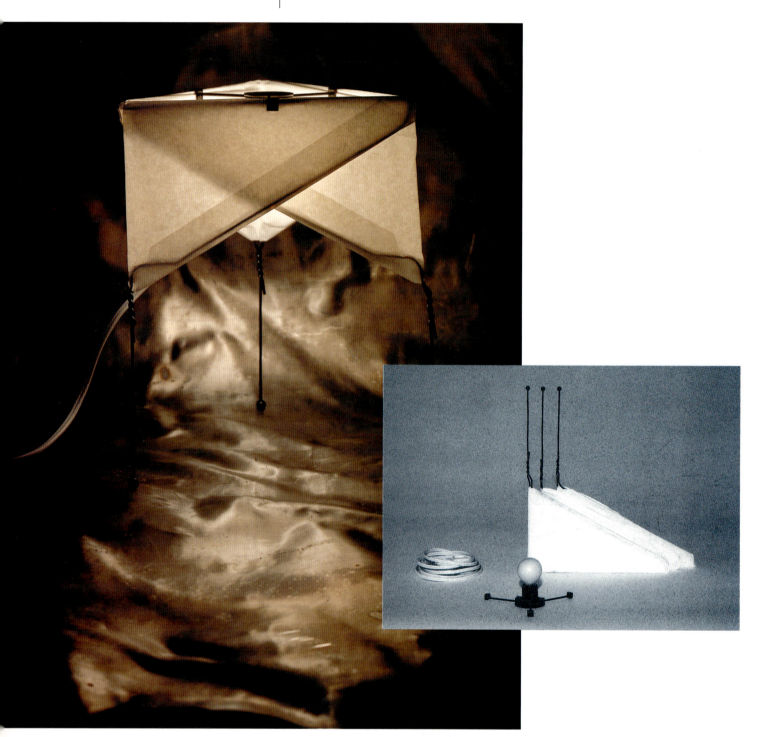

### *Ciclos*

**1985**
**Height 67 - 170cm**

Simply a glass disc suspended from the ceiling by two electrical cables, the Ciclos

incandescent or halogen ceiling light was designed by Michell De Lucchi, Milan, Italy,

for Artemide S.p.A., also of Milan.

## *Zag*

**1987**
**Height 12in x Width 17in x Depth 6in**

Using brass with a metal overlay, the designer and manufacturer Paul Ruine, of Ruine Design Assoc., New York, has created a graceful and geometrical wall sconce that cuts soft incandescent light into angular fragments. Zag is finished in either bronze, copper, nickel-chrome or aluminum.

## Henri

**1988**
6in x 12in x 9in

This homage to Magritte brilliantly deviates from the typical mass-produced lighting fixture. The lamp, suspended in what looks like thin air, is in fact attached to the wall by a thin tube; the light source is housed within a hat which is made of real felt derby for authenticity. Henri was designed and produced by Jerry Ketel of Guerilla Productions, Portland, Oregon.

# Designer Index

Client Index

## Photo Credits

pp. 15-19: T. Nacasa and
Partners
21: Idris Kolodziej
22: Terje Marthinusen
23: Stone & Steccati
24: John Montana
28: Tom Bonner
29: Kenra Izu
30: Arne Svenson
32: Robert Weindrich
37-41: Bitetto-Chimenti
42: Bill Orcutt
44: Corinne Pfister
and Tom Vack
45: Aldo Ballo
47: Aldo Ballo
49: Bitetto-Chimenti
50: Stiletto Studios
52: Bitetto-Chimenti
54: Mario Pignata Monti
56: James Evanson
57: Red Square
59-63: John Moldauer
66: Alan Linn
67: Impuls
72: Arteluce

75: Joseph Coscia,Jr.
77: Joe Davis
78: Miles Keller
79: Corinne Pfister
and Tom Vack
81-85: Alec Drummond
87: Forma Tre
88: Aldo Ballo
90: Peter Weidlein
91: Frank Linder
92: Aldo Ballo
95: Jordi Llusca
96: James Evanson
97: Corinne Pfister
and Tom Vack
99: Emilio Tremolada
103-107: Alan Linn
108: Luciano Svegliado
109: Tucker Viemeister
110: Bill Lorenz
112: Masao Ueda
113: Stefano Mosna
115: Yoram Bozaglo
118: Stefano Mosna
121: Christopher Shipley
123-127: Ian O'Leary
128: Steve Moore
129: Baker Vail
130: Bitetto-Chimenti
131: Stone & Steccati
134: Corinne Pfister
and Tom Vack
135: Floria Sigismondi
138: Giorgio Colombo
139: Beth Ludwig
141: Alex Galitzin
145-149: Andrew Dean Powell
150: Bitetto-Chimenti
152: Aldo Ballo
153: Aldo Ballo
154: Jordi Ortiz
156: Joseph Coscia, Jr.
158: Armando Diaz
159: David Morgan
162: William Deacon
163: Joseph Coscia, Jr.
173: Timothy Makepeace
177: Flos, Inc.
178: Jeffrey Mann
181: Andrea Zani
182: Mario Pignata Monti
184: Tom Bonner
185: George Fulton
187: Tom Bonner
189-193: Studio Robert
Schilder
194: Dean Powell
200: François Brunelle
202: Howard Kingsnorth
203: Aldo Ballo
205: Peter Weidlein
206: Wolfgang Karolinsky
208: George Fulton
211-215: Carlos Suarez
216: Kirti Trivedi
222: Mikio Sekita
226: R. Chepaker
227: David Potter
229: Heini Schneebeli
230: Atelier International
233-237: Kreon N. V.
238: Richard Hackett
239: Jordi Llusca
242: Alexi Harvey
244: Henk de Roij
246: Kreon N.V.
247: Joseph Coscia, Jr.
250: John Montana
251: Joe Felzman